Communication Strategies

by David Paul

THOMSON
™

Australia • Canada • Mexico • Singapore • Spain • United Kingdom • United States

Communication Strategies Teacher's Guide
by David Paul

Publishing Director: Paul Tan
ELT Director: John Lowe
Senior Development Editor: Guy de Villiers
Marketing Manager: Ian Martin

ELT Consultant: Mark Rossiter
Interior/Cover Design: Lynn Dennett
Illustrator: Ross Thomson
Printer: Seng Lee Press

For more information, contact Thomson Learning, 5 Shenton Way, #01-01 UIC Building,
Singapore 068808. Or you can visit our Internet site at http://www.thomsonlearningasia.com

For permission to use the material from this text or product, contact us by
Tel: (65) 6410-1200
Fax: (65) 6410-1208
Email: tlsg.info@thomson.com

ISBN 981-243-017-2

Printed in Singapore
3 4 5 6 06 05 04

Contents

The Stages of a Unit

There is no "right" way to use this book. Every teacher has a different style and every learning situation has its own unique requirements. The following is simply a list of suggestions for teachers using the course for the first time. The aim is not to be prescriptive, but to suggest methods that can be successfully adapted to individual teaching styles and students' needs.

1st page of a unit: Lead-in

MOVIE PICTURE

It is not absolutely necessary to use the picture. Just having it there helps draw the students into the unit. However, if you decide to use it, there are various techniques that can be used. Much depends on the level of the students, how much they know about movies, and on whether they will speak out at this stage without having any text to help them. With all these activities, the students should be encouraged to speak but not corrected too heavily.

Here are a few ideas.

Movies

Ask the students if any of them have seen the movie. If one or more have, encourage them to tell the others what they can remember about it.

Actors

If the students recognize the actors, encourage them to tell the rest of the class about them, and see if they know of any other movies they have been in. They could also say something about these other movies.

Writing first thoughts

Ask the students to write down three things that occur to them when they look at the picture. Then, in pairs, the students take turns to ask each other why they wrote down each of the three points.

Project

Have the students find out as much as possible about the movie either before the lesson or after the first lesson on the unit. They can then report back what they find. They can all give a general report, or different students can be assigned different tasks such as to find out about the plot, the actors, where it was filmed, the theme music etc...

WARM-UP QUESTIONS

Either ask individual students the questions, have them ask and answer in pairs, have them write down short answers to each question before talking, or just write down their answers and not talk at all. This is only a warm-up so don't push the students if they cannot answer soon. Encourage the students to use basic classroom language such as 'I don't understand' and 'How do I say...in English?'

If you ask a question to a student and she cannot answer, move on to another student or have other students help, but make sure you come back to that student with the same question or another question not too long afterwards, and try to ensure that the question you ask is at the right level for the student—building confidence is very important at this stage. Alternatively, simply encourage the student to say something that will give her a sense of achievement.

VOCABULARY

The words and phrases in this section will be useful throughout the unit. They are not all in the Points Of View section or any other section. They are basic words and phrases that students will need to express themselves during the course of the unit. The purposes of this section are to establish whether the students know these words and can use them, and to give the students a chance to try and make natural sentences with the ones they do not know or cannot use.

There are many ways to teach this section depending on the needs of the students and the style of the teacher. Some teachers will prefer to spend quite a lot of time on this section, and others will prefer to get through it quickly. Some teachers will go straight into the gap-fill exercise, some will get the students to make sentences with the vocabulary, and others will use games or puzzles. Some teachers will do an activity with the words from this section, and others will mix in many words from previous units. If there is time, getting the students to make sentences in fun activities, and mixing in other words from previous units is to be strongly recommended.

New words

Whatever style is used, if the students do not know a word/phrase or cannot put it into a sentence, give hints to lead them towards correct answers. If this does not work, make real sentences about yourself, famous people or subjects the students are interested in—use as much humor as possible—and then invite students to try to make similar sentences. Avoid explanation or translation. Encourage the students to guess the meaning of words/phrases from your sentences, and to consolidate their understanding through trial and error.

It is always best to encourage the students to make sentences that have as much personal meaning for them as possible (see the section on personalization).

Student-centered approach

If you decide to use a game or a student-centered activity of some kind, it is important for the teacher not to pre-teach before the activity. It is the activity that increases students' desire to know how to use the new words and phrases, and encourages them to ask the teacher for hints or sample sentences. Just go straight into the activity, starting with words you think the students may know, and wait for the activity to motivate the students to ask ques-

tions about the words they do not know or cannot use. If they do not do this, it is likely that the activity is not the right one for the class. Different classes are motivated by different activities.

When students cannot make sentences during an activity, encourage them to ask you for help. It may take time before some of the students ask for your help without hesitation, but that moment is worth planning and waiting for. When students start asking about the things they do not know, it is a sign that their natural curiosity, that may have been suppressed in many years of teacher-centered classes, is beginning to come back. And it is their involvement in the activity that motivates them to risk being curious.

When a student asks about a word she does not know, the teacher makes sample sentences that illustrate the meaning of the word without explaining the meaning. The students then make their own sentences.

Example	*New Word:* Fronkled
Student:	Fronkled! Huh! What does that mean?
Teacher:	Help her.
Other students:	Huh! Please help us!
Teacher:	Well, I'm pretty fronkled after a hard day's work (sigh). I also get real fronkled after going jogging (sigh), and extremely fronkled after teaching you! (sigh). How about you?
Student:	I'm pretty fronkled after studying English.

SOME POSSIBLE VOCABULARY ACTIVITIES

One or more of these activities can be used:

Straightforward approach

The students make sentences with these words and phrases either orally around the class, with or without pair practice first, or in writing.

The Stages of a Unit

Usage

Ask the students to suggest when we use each word/phrase either before or after making a sentence. If there is time, they can first do this in pairs before reporting to the whole class.

Synonyms and definitions

Ask the students to think of synonyms or definitions of some or all of the words/phrases. This will not be easy for some of the words/phrases so it is best to write down selected words/phrases on the board. The students can also work on this in pairs first.

Match the synonym or definition

Give the students synonyms or definitions and have the students guess which synonym/definition goes with each word.

Word association

The students think of other words or ideas they associate with some or all of the words/phrases. This can be done as a brainstorming session with the whole class with or without pair practice first.

Adding more words

The students think of more words/phrases which they associate with the theme of the unit and that could be added to the list. This can also be done with or without pair practice first.

What's the missing word?

Write sentences on the board with a space for one of the words from the list. The students guess what the word is. If possible, write sentences that mean something to you (i.e. not ones about 'John' or 'Mary' but about you or people/things you are genuinely interested in). This is a very gentle activity which can work well with a new class.

Race

In pairs or teams the students race to work out definitions of each of the words in the list.

Timed talk

Students try to talk without hesitation for a fixed amount of time (e.g. 2 mins) on a word from the list. This can be done as a game where a successful student wins points for her team.

Making corrections

Make incorrect sentences with the words/phrases and have the students work out what the mistakes are. An alternative is to give them a choice of sentences, one of which is correct.

Odd one out

Make groups of words (usually three) and get the students to decide which one is the odd one out and give a reason. It's not necessary to choose words that have an obvious connection.

Questioning

The teacher writes a list of sample questions on the board:

Example: Where can we find a _____ ?
Why do some people _____ ?
How many times a day do you
    see a _____ ?
Who often _____ ?
Where do _____ come from?
+ 3 more questions of your choice.

The students are in pairs. One student asks the questions and the other answers, and they then switch roles. The teacher throws out a word from a list—if it is an adjective or adverb, the teacher puts it with a noun or verb, or gets the students to do this if they can.

Make a story

The students try to make a story that connects as many of the words together as possible. This is usually best done in pairs or teams.

Card activities

The students have cards for words/phrases from the present list and from previous units. The words from previous units should be for any words/phrases the students found difficult or needed more practice with, not just the words in the vocabulary sections. Ideally, these cards should be made by each student, but this may or may not be feasible. If not, the teacher should make them and, where possible, each student can have a set.

N.B. It can help students a lot to have these cards even if there are no card activities in the class.

Whether or not students have personal sets, they can play card games such as Snap, Concentration (needs two sets), UNO (with numbers on the cards) or any game the students like. Each time they play a card, or, if this slows down the game too much, each time something special and positive (not a penalty) happens such as winning a trick, they make a sentence with the card they have played.

They can also play board games such as Snakes and Ladders and turn over the top card from a pile either before throwing the dice or before something special happens such as going up a ladder.

Grid games

Put the words/phrases from the current unit and previous units in grids and play games such as Bingo, Tic Tac Toe, Tiddleywinks or throwing games. The students make sentences with the words/phrases either each turn or when something special happens in the game (such as when a student wins Bingo she makes a sentence with each word in her winning line).

(a) Bingo

Dictate words that students write down anywhere on a bingo grid, putting one word in each square. Each of these words is also put in a box. The students take turns to draw a word from the box and call it out. A student that completes a line in any direction calls out 'Bingo'. A student that gets bingo has to make a sentence with each of the words in the line.

(b) Tic Tac Toe

Write words in each square of a Tic Tac Toe grid either on the board or on pieces of paper for the students to play with in pairs. The most difficult words should be in the center of the grid.

An improvement on the original Tic Tac Toe game is to use a 4x4 or 5x5 grid. The students are in two teams, and take turns to place an O or X in the grid. A team gets a point for getting three Os or Xs in a row, either horizontally, vertically or diagonally. An O or X later in the game can often be worth two or three points.

(c) Tiddleywinks

Make a tiddleywinks board with a word in each square, and allocate points to each square according to the difficulty of the word. Students flick a counter or coin onto the board and collect points.

Throwing

Use something that sticks to the board, such as a sticky ball, an arrow shot from a bow etc... Write words/phrases in a target on the board. These can be conventional targets, grid games, pictures of animals, or something else that is visually stimulating. When students hit a word, they make a sentence and get points for that word, try to get a line of words etc...

Another kind of throwing game is to play some version of basketball where the students throw a soft ball into a basket, a dice into a box etc... and make a sentence with a word/phrase each time they throw or whenever they succeed.

Ladders

Draw a ladder on the board that has clear stages. The stages used depend on the kinds of students in the class. With some classes, the bottom of the ladder could be things like spiders or cockroaches, and the top an alien. With other students, the ladder could reflect the grades of management in their company.

The students are in teams and take turns to make sentences with words/phrases. They move up one stage of the ladder either after making a sentence (or a certain number of sentences) or after doing some additional task such as throwing a dice and getting a 5 or 6 or throwing a soft ball into a basket.

Board activities

(a) Spaces

Put the students in teams. Think of a sentence

The Stages of a Unit

that includes one of the target words (in a mixed level class, a student with higher English ability can do this) and write it on the board, putting a dash instead of each letter in the sentence. The students take turns to call out a letter. If the letter is in the sentence, the teacher writes down the letter above each dash that corresponds to that letter. After each correct guess, the team can try to guess the sentence.

This is a variation of Hangman, but in fact any scoring system can be used. For example, after guessing the sentence a student can try to throw a dice into a box.

(b) Mixed up sentences

Make sentences using a few of the words, and then scatter them around the board (or on handouts). Say how many sentences there are. The students try to separate the sentences out from the mass of words.

(c) Telepathy

Write about 4 sentences on the board. Each sentence contains one of the target words (humorous sentences work best). One student stands in front of the class, secretly chooses a sentence, then closes her eyes and tries to send the sentence to the other students telepathically. The other students close their eyes and try to receive the sentence. The students then say which sentence they chose, and see if it is correct. They then do the same activity in groups, taking turns to send out the sentence, and getting points for receiving it correctly. The teacher gradually changes the sentences, using more of the words.

Gap-fill exercise

The gap-fill exercise below the vocabulary section can either be used for consolidation after the students have done one or more activities with the vocabulary, or it can be used at an earlier stage to assess the students' understanding of the vocabulary. Each student can do the exercise individually, in pairs, or the whole class can work together on finding the possible answers. Even if the students first work by themselves, it is best to bring the class together and ask them to suggest answers.

Please note that more than one of the

words/phrases in the vocabulary section may fit in some of the gaps. This is deliberate. The students need to get used to the idea that English is not mathematics with clear right or wrong answers. If the students are not clear about any of the answers, it may be helpful to practice a few more personalized sentences together.

Finally, ask the students to answer the question below the gap-fill exercise. They can also do this activity individually, in pairs or as a class. Encourage them to think of people, free time activities, things that happened to them in the past etc… and think of words that would be useful to describe these topics. They may need to use dictionaries to look for new words, or get help from you or the other students.

MIND MAP

Ask the students to look at the mind map in the unit just to get a general idea of how a mind map works, and to get some specific ideas. Then start a mind map on the board using one of the starting points suggested below the map in the book, or another related topic.

Base the board mind map around one of the more confident students. For example write '5 years ago' in the center of the mind map, and invite her to say or write ideas that spring to mind when she thinks of '5 years ago'. Encourage the other students to help her by making suggestions.

If one of the ideas connected to '5 years ago' is 'went to new York', encourage her to say or write things that spring to mind when she thinks about that trip to New York. Either you or her writes these ideas on the board, branching off from 'went to New York'. After the map is finished, ask the student to talk about '5 years ago', using the map as a reference point, going through each train of thought, and elaborating on it when possible. All the students then work out their own mind maps, and talk through them with each other in pairs, in groups, or to the class if the class is small.

These mind maps can also form the basis for personalized writing either in the lesson or for homework. The students write short essays using their maps as frameworks. Whether or not this is possible will probably depend on the nature of the course, but this kind of practice is invaluable in helping the students clarify their thoughts and develop the ability to express themselves in English.

2nd page of a unit: Points Of View

POINTS OF VIEW

General considerations

The students can listen to the discussion on the audio program or read by the teacher or other students, or read the dialogue, or both.

Listening

Using the audio program in class

(a) If students are taking an intensive course or having a class almost every day, using the audio program regularly can lead to a distinct improvement in students' ability to listen to English.

(b) If students have only one or two lessons a week and little exposure to English between classes, there is little evidence to suggest that listening to an audio program will make much difference to the students' ability to listen to English, so in these kinds of learning situations it is more important to encourage students to listen to English for a short time every day out of class. It may help if each student has a copy of the audio program with this book, and is encouraged to listen to it in the car, every evening before going to sleep etc...

So, when lessons are infrequent, if the audio program is used in class it is more to provide variety, to stimulate the students' interest, to learn how to focus on particular aspects of the conversation, and to encourage the students to use the audio program at home and give them the confidence to do so, rather than because it is going to make much difference to their listening ability.

(c) For teachers who are not native speakers, using the audio program in class may give the students exposure to more natural intonation and pronunciation. If the teacher is a native speaker, using the audio program may give the students exposure to a wider variety of pronunciation.

(d) If the text is easy for the students, it is more challenging for them to listen to the discussion with books closed than to read it. They can then answer comprehension questions or manipulate the language (see below) before looking at the text.

Things to consider

(a) Listening to an audio program is often a passive classroom activity, and encourages the students to be followers rather than active participants in the class. With motivated classes, this may not matter at all, but with other classes passive activities of this kind can undermine the work we have been doing to get the students to be active learners.

Using the activities suggested below helps reduce this feeling. However, even when we do many interesting activities, listening to an audio program can easily feel like an activity the teacher wants students to do, rather than something they are emotionally involved in. With some highly motivated classes, it does not matter very much if a lesson feels like a lesson, but with other

The Stages of a Unit

students this feeling can have a very negative effect on the effectiveness of the class.

(b)   In some situations, particularly in language schools, students may feel that 'listening' is something they can do at home, and they want to spend as much time as possible practicing 'speaking'. This is particularly the case if they have classes only once or twice a week.

Reading

The students can either read the dialogue after listening to it, or they can read it instead of listening to it. Some teachers believe that silent reading is important, and others believe it is important for students to practice reading aloud so the teacher can help them improve their intonation and pronunciation. Which is right? Perhaps it partly depends on what the students want to do, and it certainly depends on whether they need to practice reading aloud and improve their pronunciation.

But there is a more fundamental issue. Whatever the method, the key question is 'Are the students involved in what they are doing?' If they regard reading as a rather flat classroom activity, then get it over with as quickly as possible, or interrupt it and bring it alive with some of the activities suggested below.

It can also help to encourage students to read with dramatic intonation. For example, if students take the roles of the characters, you could ask one student to read very sadly, and another to read angrily. Another similar method is to get the students to read the dialogue to each other in pairs, and while they are reading, hold up adverb cards (or even better, have a student do this) such as 'fast', 'slowly', 'romantically', 'quietly', 'loudly', 'angrily' etc... The students read with the emotion written on the card or called out by you or a student. Keep changing the cards. The whole point is to get some emotion into the activity. But, of course, with many classes this may not be necessary, or the students may be too self conscious and not ready to do this kind of thing.

Activities

It can help a lot to have activities before, during and after listening to or reading the discussion. These activities draw the students into the discussion or the particular language in this section, make it more alive and relevant, and help the students internalize the patterns more deeply so they can use them actively. The activities marked * are in each of the 'listening/reading worksheets' in this Teacher's Book. The other activities are alternatives:

Before listening or reading

Warm-up questions *

Ask the students questions which are directly connected with the discussion in this section, or put them into pairs and encourage them to answer each question. An alternative is for them to first write down their answers and then discuss each other's answers in pairs.

Anticipation gap-fill *

The students are given sentences from the discussion with one or more words missing. They try and guess what the words might be before listening to or reading the discussion. While they are reading or listening, they can see whether they were correct or not.

Natural conversation

Chat with the students about the topic. During this natural conversation, either ask questions using patterns in the text, or help them express what they want to say using some of the words or patterns in the text. Try to make this as natural as possible.

Pre-reading/listening questions

Ask the students questions for the students to answer while reading or listening to the text. It is usually best to write these questions on the board unless the text is quite easy for the students.

Characters

Tell the students the topic of the discussion and who is taking part, and ask them what they expect each character to think. This works better later in the book when the students have gotten to know the characters.

Mixing things up

Put sentences from the discussion into word puzzles on the board for the students to try and solve with their books closed.

(a) For example (mixing letters)
TOMOKO SKILE OPLEPE HTTA REA BOSLECIA
JIN-SOOK SKILE OPLEPE HTTA REA TIUQE

(b) For example (mixing words)
likes are that sociable people Tomoko
people Jin-Sook quiet are that likes

The students then see if they were right when they listen to or read the discussion.

Clouds

Put words in one or more clouds on the board. One way to select the words is to choose the key words in a character's opinion. The students then try and see how the words could be combined.
For example:

Game

Choose a mixture of easy and difficult words or patterns from the discussion and play a game such as one of those suggested in the vocabulary section.

While listening or reading

*Listening/reading for gist ***
Dictate or write questions for the students to try and answer while listening or reading. These questions should not be about specific points in the text, but should be more general and elicit their general impressions.

*Noticing words ***
Give the students a list of words or expressions, and ask them to circle the ones they hear or see.

*Reading search ***
Have the students search the text for words from definitions, synonyms, words which collocate with those in the text, words beginning with a certain letter etc…

Reading race
Say a word and have the students race to find it. The winning student/team then puts the word into one or more different sentences.

Manipulating language
The students first listen to and/or read the whole discussion, and then listen or read again in short sections. Encourage them to manipulate the language during these pauses. Here are some techniques:

(a) Rephrasing
See if the students can suggest other ways of expressing an idea in the discussion. Some of the ways this can be done are:

Give a starting prompt
Sentence in text: I prefer to have friends who stand back.
Prompts from teacher: She'd rather …
She thinks it's …

Ask for alternative words/phrases
Sentence in text: I couldn't go out with anybody who wasn't sensitive.
Teacher: Change 'go out with'.

The Stages of a Unit

Students: She couldn't date anybody that wasn't sensitive.
She couldn't have a boy-friend that wasn't sensitive.
She couldn't have a relation-ship with anybody that wasn't sensitive.

It may be necessary to give hints and prompts to elicit these alternative expressions.

(b) Personalization

Have the students make personalized sentences using the patterns in the text (see the section on personalization). The patterns in the text have been selected for their transferability so personalization is likely to be an effective way to manipulate the language in the text.

A variation on this is for the students to read or listen to sections of the discussion and immediately give their opinions. This can either be done after first reading or listening to the whole discussion all the way through, or before this happens. It mainly depends on the level of the students and whether you want to build confidence or challenge the students.

(c) Synonyms/word association

See if the students can think of synonyms for words in the text or ask them to think of other words they associate with a word in the text.

(d) Collocations

See if the students can suggest other words that collocate with words or phrases in the text (see the 'Collocation sets' section).

(e) Register

See if the students can suggest how to make an expression more or less polite.

(f) Comprehension personalization in chains

See below for a full explanation. These chains can be set up during pauses in the text so as to immediately make the patterns relevant and personal.

After listening or reading

General questions *

The students write or ask each other general questions on the text.

It is best to avoid questions that only get the students to give short answers or where they have a 50% chance of getting the correct answer. Some examples are:

Question: Does she like people that are sociable?
Student: Yes.

Question: She likes students that are sociable. True or false?
Student: True.

These methods tell us very little about whether the students have understood.

Correct these statements *

The students correct the false statements in the worksheets.

Alternatively, make correct and incorrect statements from the text and have the students correct you when you make mistakes. One way to do this is to close the book or appear to only half listen to the audio program, and pretend you have forgotten much of what was said in the discussion, or genuinely forget—the more genuine your mistakes sound to the students, the more likely it will be that they will speak out and correct you. It is best to use as much humor as possible.

It is worth noting that it is generally good to be a fallible teacher and make mistakes to get the students to speak out more. It is natural for any of us to be intimidated in a conversation if we feel the other person knows much more than us, and this is how most students feel about their teachers. Looked at from this point of view, it is quite natural that so many students do not speak out spontaneously in class but happily do so when they are with their friends. Being a fallible teacher is one way to deal with this problem.

Teacher:	Now what was it Tomoko said? I think she said she likes people who are sociable and quiet. Yes, that's right.
Student(s):	No.
Teacher:	What's the matter?
Student(s):	She likes people that talk a lot.
Teacher:	Are you sure?
Student(s):	Yes!
Teacher:	I must have a bad memory. And Tomoko thinks it's cool to be … etc…

It can be a lot of fun to be the absent-minded teacher. It is a role you can maintain for much of the lesson, and it encourages a lot more activity and spontaneity even from quite shy classes.

The students can also do the same thing in pairs. One student pretending to be very absent minded, and the other student correcting her.

Comprehension/personalization questions *

The students can write answers or ask each other the questions in the worksheets, or they can practice in chains around the class. Here are some examples of chains:

(a) Basic technique

Teacher:	What kind of people does Tomoko like?
Student 1:	She likes people that are sociable.
Teacher:	You … (gestures for the student to ask another student)
Student 1:	What kind of people do you like?
Student 2:	I like people that have a sense of humor.

You can just leave it at that, or the students can ask each other in a chain around the class.

(b) Starting from a negative answer

Teacher:	Does she feel comfortable when she's with people that are dangerous?
Student 1:	No, she doesn't.
Teacher:	When …? (gestures for student 1 to

	ask student 2)
Student 1:	When does she feel comfortable?
Student 2:	When she's with people that are quiet …
Teacher:	You? (gestures for student 2 to ask student 3)
Student 2:	When do you feel comfortable?
Student 3:	I feel comfortable when …

Once the students have got used to the technique, they can ask the initial question. They ask questions which are absurd or obviously not true (humor works best), so as to elicit a negative answer.

Pair checking

One student looks at the text and asks questions about it to the other student. They then reverse roles. If the students are used to the kind of practice in the 'Comprehension/personalization' section above, they can follow each answer with a personalized example. For example:

Student 1:	When does she feel comfortable?
Student 2:	When she's with people that are quiet.
Student 1:	When do you feel comfortable?
Student 2:	When I'm with people who have a good sense of humor.

Remembering

Get the students to close their books and see how much they can remember about what each of the characters said. The idea is to focus on meaning not on the exact language used.

One variation on this is for a student from one team to speak for one minute, and then to quickly point to a student from another team to continue speaking. If a student, with help from her team, stops talking or runs out of things to say, the team loses.

Summarizing/interviewing

Ask the students to summarize the arguments of one or more of the characters. They can do this as a class—helping each other—or individually. They can also summarize in pairs.

The Stages of a Unit

A way of doing the same kind of thing in a more involved and imaginative way is for one student in a pair to be a TV interviewer or newspaper reporter and the other student to be one of the characters in the story. They can reverse roles, with the student who was the interviewer becoming the other character in the discussion. The interviewers can ask questions directly related to the text or, if the students are ready for this, they can get into their roles more and take the interviews in any directions they like.

3rd page of a unit: Practice and Discussion

PERSONALIZATION

Personalization is used extensively at every stage of a unit and this section is a way to consolidate the students' ability to personalize some of the patterns encountered in the previous section. It is also a stepping stone between the text and the discussion at the bottom of the page.

The students practice the sentences either in pairs or around the class. They should be encouraged to give any examples that are true for them. Each student should have a chance to answer every question. It is important for them to practice orally at this stage, and they should not be restricted by the theme of the unit or the discussion in the text.

Some students will give simple answers and others will be more ambitious. At this stage of the lesson, it is best to encourage students to be as ambitious as they can, but it is important to know their limit and not push them too far.

It may take practice before all the students are comfortable with this kind of activity—some of the sentences require quite a lot of imagination. Give prompts, hints and examples about yourself if necessary, but back away as the students get the idea.

The questions in this section are only a starting point. If you have noticed any patterns the students seem to have difficulty with either in this unit or in previous units, you can add them to this section either by writing extra questions on the board or allocating more questions individually.

It is best to keep a notebook for jotting down patterns the students find difficult. In many situations it may be best to make a mental note of a problem and write it down during a natural break rather than interrupt the flow of an activity or discussion. This can also be done at other stages of a lesson.

Definition

The word 'personalization' has been used a number of times so far. When students personalize words or structures, this generally means they use these words and structures in sentences about themselves.

Example: I like people that are sociable.

Rather than fictional people:

Example: John (or Mary) like people that are sociable.

It can also mean the students make sentences about their family, friends, neighborhood, country, books/movies they like, topics of conversation that get them excited etc...

The emotional dimension of 'personalization' is particularly important. Students should be encouraged to talk or write about subjects they have a genuine feeling about. If it is not important to a student whether her brother likes swimming, then to say 'My brother likes swimming' is not really a personalized sentence.

One of our major roles as teachers is to discover the world in which our students really live. We can then encourage and prompt them to give as many examples as possible from this world.

To find out what is important for our students, it may help to give a questionnaire to a new class. The kind of questions asked will depend on the age and level of the students, but here is an example of what can be done. It is sometimes best to ask students to write in their native language—this may give you more useful information.

Questionnaire

1. Family
Give information about each member of your family (name, age, occupation), and write a few sentences about each of them.

2. Friends
Give information about two or three of your best friends, and write a few sentences about each of them.

3. Books
Name the two books you like best, and say why you like them.
Name one book you don't like and say why.

4. Movies
Name the two movies you like best, and say why you like them.
Name one movie you don't like and say why.

5. Sport
Name your favorite sport and say why you like it.
Name a sport you don't like and say why.

6. Sundays
Name two things you like to do on Sundays and say why.
Name one thing you don't like to do on Sundays and say why.

7. Topics
Name one topic you enjoy talking about and say why.
Name one topic you don't enjoy talking about and say why.

8. Respect
Name two people you respect and say why.
Name one person you don't respect and say why.

9. Work
Name one job you would like to do in future and say why.
Name one job you wouldn't like to do and say why.

10. Ambitions
Name two things (not work) you would like to do in future and say why.
Name one thing you wouldn't want to do in future and say why.

11. Routine
Name two things you have to do almost every day that you don't like.
Name two things you have to do almost every day that you like very much.

12. Home
Do you like your house/apartment? Say why.
Where would you ideally like to live? Why?

The Stages of a Unit

You can get a lot of information from a questionnaire like this. It is not just the facts. It is often what is implied that is just as important as the opinions themselves.

Examples:

If a student says she respects somebody because he's tall and generous, then there's a good chance the constructs 'tall-short' and 'mean-generous' may be important for that student.

If a student says the person he most respects is his mother and the thing he most likes doing is cooking dinner, you can begin to get a better picture of at least one of the worlds that is important for him, and can put examples into that world.

This is only a starting point. As you get to know the students better, you will modify and often completely change your ideas about what's important for them. It can take some time before we can really get into the world of each of our students and, just as importantly, for them to get into our world, but whether we can achieve this or not will often dictate the success or failure of our classes. The questionnaire is just an initial step on the road to understanding, which, of course, never ends.

JOKES

(also applies to the jokes on the other pages)

Humor is an essential part of any lesson for so many reasons. It motivates and increases the students emotional involvement in the lesson. Emotion is a central part of learning, and plays an even more important role in increasing retention. So often, students remember a language point because they associate it with an enjoyable or humorous situation. Having jokes on a page also draws students into the material by making it much more approachable. A page that feels like 'studying' is so often pushed aside, both during the lesson and at home after the lesson.

Using the jokes in class
STEP 1

Ask the students questions either to help them understand the jokes or to check they understand the language. For example, if the joke depends on a pun, ask them to guess the two meanings of the key word.

Example:	"Did you miss me when I was away?" "Were you away?"
Teacher:	Did she miss him? How do you know?
If this fails:	Did she notice he has been away? So did she miss him?

STEP 2

Have the students make personalized sentences (see the section on personalization) using the key words/phrases in the joke dialogue. Either all the students or a few individual students can do this orally, or they can all try to write personalized sentences.

Example:	Who do you miss? (ask each other) What places do you miss? (ask each other) Does your father/mother/ husband/wife go away sometimes? Where does he/she go? (ask each other)

DISCUSSION

This section is what the previous sections have been leading up to. By now, the students should, at least potentially, have the tools to discuss the questions in this section and others like them. They should now be given free rein to speak and speak and speak, and it is often a good idea to add more discussion questions to the ones in the book. They can do this as a class or in pairs. It depends on the number of students and whether they all speak out or not. Larger classes or classes that include students that don't speak out a lot should do these discussion questions in pairs.

In each unit, there are three 'Discussion strategies' for the students to use during the discussions. It is best to write these on the board before the discussion starts. It may also help to write expressions from previous units that you would like the students to use, and any key vocabulary or expressions from the current unit or previous units you would like the students to practice.

To get the maximum benefit from this discussion time, it is necessary to be careful about the following points:

Domination by individual students

One of the main problems in many classes is that discussions are dominated by one or two students. It is essential to do everything possible to prevent this from happening, otherwise some of the other students can easily lose confidence or speak out much less than they would if the dominant students were not there. The most subtle way is simply to put all the students in pairs and make sure a dominant student is not talking with a student that can be intimidated. Another way is to direct questions to individuals that aren't participating as much.

Partiality

Another problem is that we may identify more with students that speak out a lot or have opinions that are close to our own, and this can intimidate other students or make them feel excluded. This is often subtle. The students that aren't included may not say anything. They may just become quieter, politer or find an excuse for not attending the class. To avoid this, we need to step back and take a long professional look at the role we are playing in the class.

Teacher domination

A third problem is that we may dominate discussions, even when it seems we are hardly speaking. It is very likely that we will win any discussion. We may think this is because our argument is wonderful and everybody is agreeing with us, but it may simply be because we haven't really given enough openings for students to express their real opinions, or encouraged them to say things that

are difficult to express in English. Students do often want to know what we think, and giving our opinion is an important part of making human contact with the students. It is good if students can get into our world as much as we get into theirs. However, there are really only three occasions on which we should give our opinions:

(1) When the students aren't speaking a lot or only making superficial comments, we may need to provoke or play devil's advocate so as to add some spice to the discussions. If students are only saying superficial things, they will tend to use easy and familiar patterns. If students are worked up and trying to say something important to them, it is much more likely that they will search for new ways of saying things and hopefully find that using some of the words and structures introduced earlier in the unit can help them express themselves.

(2) After the students have been given a lot of chance to express themselves.

(3) When students ask us genuine questions. This is the most difficult one. We want to answer their questions, but we mustn't do so too convincingly otherwise we'll have too big an influence on the subsequent discussion, and we must put the ball back in their court as soon as possible. A brief, genuine answer followed by a return question is often the best policy.

Students don't use new words and structures

The students may talk a lot, but not try to use the words and structures they have been learning in the previous stages of the unit. Their English ability may not really be moving forward very much. This is usually because one of the previous sections of the unit has not been done thoroughly enough. This does not mean that every activity suggested so far has to be done in every class—it

The Stages of a Unit

depends very much on the class and time available—but if students are not using the target language during the discussions, it is worth looking back at the previous stages of the unit and thinking about which section might need to be emphasized more. It is also important to ask whether the students have been emotionally involved enough in the previous stages of the unit—without this emotional dimension to learning, the new language is less likely to be used spontaneously in the discussions.

With some classes, an added incentive is for students to award themselves points for including particular words and structures in their discussions. Before the discussion begins, write the words and structures in a list on the board with points next to each of them. You can award more points for words/structures that are more difficult or ones you particularly want the students to practice. This list should include words/structures from earlier units, and ones that are not in the book but the students have had difficulty with.

4th page of a unit: Activities

FOLLOW-UP QUESTIONS

These are usually quick activities done in pairs. However, if necessary, start by asking quick questions around the class and immediately follow up each answer with another question:

For example: (unit 1)

Teacher:	What kind of people do you like?
Student 1:	I like people that are quiet.
Teacher:	What do you like doing with your quiet friends?
Teacher:	What are you fed up with?
Student 2:	I'm fed up with getting up early every day.
Teacher:	Why do you have to get up early?

Once the students have been loosened up, go straight into the activity.

Reporting back

It often helps if individual pairs report back to the rest of the class. One student can report back on what the other student has said or they can demonstrate a sample dialogue. If students know this may happen, they are likely to concentrate harder during the pair work activity. Avoid putting students in a situation where they are likely to fail. Whatever you ask the students to report should be something they are capable of reporting with some help from you.

ROLE PLAY

These activities can also be done fairly quickly. If necessary, help one pair demonstrate each activity to the rest of the students. If they are not sitting in a place where the other students can see what's going on, the pair can be brought out to the front of the class. It is important not to get the model pair to model a precise dialogue you want the students to practice or even to go too far into any kind of practice. The model pair should do just enough to get the others started and give them a general idea of what they could do.

Many of the role plays give students the option of being themselves or a famous person. In these cases, each student chooses who they will be and tells the other student in their pair. They then each write down questions they would like to ask each other. First one student plays the role of asking questions, and then the other.

Even in those role plays where there are no reporters, each student should have some time to prepare things to say and questions to ask. They then practice the role play, and may give a demonstration in front of the other students.

SITUATIONS

In this section, the students cover a wide range of everyday situations, and learn and practice everyday language patterns that intermediate students may not be familiar with or be able to use. The example patterns given in the book are just a starting point. Every teacher has their own favorite everyday expressions and these should be introduced as well, bearing in mind that we can never be sure where our students will use their English in the future, so the expressions should preferably be ones they can use all over the world.

The situations and suggested patterns in these sections are deliberately a little dramatic and sometimes humorous. The emphasis is on getting the students emotionally involved in what they are doing. At the same time, we need to realize that many of our students may be intimidated by elaborate role plays and hesitate to use exaggerated gestures. The situations in this book have been designed to be achievable by most classes and in most cultures.

STEP 1

Lead into each situation with a brief warm-up activity such as one of the following:

(a) Brainstorming

Brainstorm using the questions in the student's book or other similar questions. You can do this with the whole class, or have the students brainstorm in pairs and then report their ideas to you. Sometimes the students will want to look at the book for ideas. Let them do this. It means they are choosing to open the book and study the examples there, and this is the kind of attitude we want to encourage.

Target situation: Telephone B and ask him/her out to dinner etc...

Teacher: Think of things we often say on the telephone

Students: Hello.
This is ...

Could I speak to ...?
I'm sorry, she's busy. etc...
(write down each pattern on the board)

Add touches to the expressions the students suggest to make them more natural.

Student A: I'm sorry, she's busy.

Teacher: Do we stop there?
I'm sorry, she's busy ... (gesture to continue. If necessary, point to your watch)

Student B: I'm sorry, she's busy. Please call again at 3 o'clock.

Teacher: Yes. That's good. Or, I'm sorry, she's busy at the moment. Please call again after 3 o'clock.

(b) Questioning

Isolate some of the target patterns you would like the students to focus on and put them in questions to the students.

Target pattern: I'm thinking of ...

Teacher: What are you thinking of doing this weekend?
What are you thinking of doing over Christmas?
etc...

If the students cannot answer, get them to ask you the question. Give natural answers until they guess the meaning of the question and can try and give their own answers.

After throwing out a few questions in this way, write the framework of the questions on the board, and have the students ask and answer in pairs.

(c) Personalized sentences

Write down target patterns on the board or

The Stages of a Unit

throw them out to the class one at a time. The students make personalized sentences in writing or orally as a class or in pairs.

Example: I spend all my time ...
I never help ... etc...

(d) Puzzles
Put some of the target patterns into a puzzle.

Target patterns: Why doesn't it have a roof?
Are you sure it's not necessary?
I can't pay as much as that.

Scatter the words from these three sentences all over the board. If appropriate, put them inside a cloud or simple picture. The students try to separate out the three sentences.

(e) Mini-situations
Act out a mini-situation to lead into a more complex situation.

Target situation: Apologizing

Teacher: (bump into one of the students—clearly on purpose)
Oh, I'm extremely sorry! It was an accident.

Student: (teacher helps students say these kinds of expressions)
No problem.
Never mind. etc...

STEP 2
The students do the activity in the book. There are many ways of doing this, and most teachers will have their own ways of dealing with these kinds of situations. Here are some possibilities:

(a) Model pair
With a large class, bring a pair of students out to the front of the class. With a small class, the pair you choose can stay in their seats. Say which student is A and which student is B, either outline their role to them or have them read through their roles, and go straight into the situation and see what happens.

Encourage the students to try, and help them to improve the expressions they use, wherever possible leading them towards the patterns in the book or other patterns you think are important. The important thing is to encourage them to get into the role and just speak.

The model pair shouldn't demonstrate for too long, and they certainly shouldn't practice a dialogue for the other students to copy exactly. The idea is to continue long enough for the other students to understand what they need to do, but not longer than this.

Then all the students do the activity in pairs with books open, using the sample patterns to help them. Walk around the class, encouraging the students to speak out and say what they want to say rather than copy what the model students said.

(b) Mime
Either you mime the roles of both A and B, or use a model pair helping them with each mime until they get the idea. Either you or the students mime a stage of the situation and encourage the other students to suggest what to say.

Example: One student walks into a shop, opening the door (make sound of bell), point to the shop assistant and gesture to ask what the assistant says. The students may suggest things like 'May I help you?' and if you want them to learn new patterns, you could throw out alternatives such as 'What can I do for you?'

After going through a situation like this, do it again completely silently—the students to do all the talking. One way is to divide the class into two teams, one team work together to play A's role, and the other team play B's role.

The students then do the activity in pairs with books open.

(c) Working alone

Divide the class into pairs or groups. Each pair/group looks at the situation in the book and tries to work out what to do. Then ask some pairs or groups to demonstrate the dialogue they have come up with. The idea is to let the students try and understand and think through what to do by themselves. With some classes, it can be fun to make the demonstrations into a contest.

STEP 3

For some classes, there may be no time, or it may be unnecessary, to do more with these situations. However, with other classes it would be best to extend and widen the patterns practiced so far. Here are some ideas for what can be done:

(a) Related situations

The students search for what to say in situations that are somehow related to the one in the book.

Sample situation: Telephone B to ask him/her out.

Teacher: Asking somebody out is one kind of telephone conversation. What other kinds of telephone conversations do we have?

Students: (pairs of students making lists or brainstorming as a whole class) Arranging a place to meet. Getting train information. etc...

Pairs of students choose one or more of these dialogues and practice the situations, asking the teacher for help when they need it.

(b) Extension of structures

Write key patterns on the board. These can be the patterns from the book or other patterns that have come out of the previous practice.

Ask the students to make other sentences using these patterns, sometimes providing hints by suggesting other kinds of situations in which they can be used. Alternatively, put the students in pairs, and give them a list of situations to use each pattern in.

Target pattern: 'If you have time, you could ...'

Example substitutions: enough money
a lot of energy

Example situations for pairs:
I hate my job
I have a broken heart
My dog doesn't like me
etc...

5th page of a unit: Further Activities

COLLOCATION SETS

Whenever our students learn new words, it is important for them to learn the other words these words usually combine with. Many combinations of words are possible but some pairs of words occur together very frequently. Knowing the most frequent collocations of a word can help make a student's English a lot more natural.

In this section, there are some common collocations of words related to the theme of the unit. Some example sentences are given, and the aim is for the students to make sentences using the other collocations. They can do this individually, in pairs or as a class.

If the students make mistakes, give some examples, preferably personalized sentences or sentences about subjects that will arouse their interest.

The Stages of a Unit

After listening to your examples, they can try again to make their own sentences.

To consolidate their understanding, it can help a lot to do one of the fun activities mentioned in the Vocabulary section. For example, pairs of words that collocate from the current unit and previous units could be put in a Tic Tac Toe grid on the board and the students either play the game in a straightforward way or throw or shoot something at the squares on the board in order to put an O or X in that square. Whenever they choose or hit a square, they make a sentence with the word combination in that square.

SPEECHES

The aim of this section is to give students more confidence and practice in speaking in front of others, either formally or informally, and in helping them to present well-ordered arguments.

Either use the topics suggested, other topics you think are appropriate for a particular class, or any topic related to the theme of the unit that is chosen by each student. This last method can be particularly motivating for some classes.

Students should be given time to prepare their speeches. If necessary, brainstorm the topic with the class before the students start to prepare. Each student then makes a speech, the length of which depends on the number of students in the class and the time available.

Some teachers prefer to allocate a fixed time in each lesson for selected students to make short speeches they have prepared before the lesson. This can also work well.

Questioning

It can be a good idea to have a short question time after a speech, with other students asking questions to the person who made the speech. If students don't ask very probing questions, tell individual students they are newspaper reporters or TV interviewers, and ask them to write down questions while they are listening to the speech. The students then ask these questions, in their role as reporters/interviewers, after the speech.

Interruption game

Each student prepares a speech. Set an alarm without telling the students what time it is set for. One student starts to make their speech. A student can interrupt whenever another student pauses. The student that is talking when the alarm goes off gets a point.

Pauses

Students have to speak for as long as possible. If they pause, they must use a natural pause strategy. If they pause without doing this, their time is finished. The student who speaks the longest is the winner. A variation of this is to allow other students to ask questions to try and throw the student out of her stride.

Example pause strategies:
> repeating the previous statement
> rhetorical questions
> Well ...
> uh ...
> It's like this ...
> You know what I mean ...
> You see ...
> etc...

EXTRA EXPRESSIONS

There is some debate about whether students should learn idioms or not. There is research that seems to show that we hardly ever use many of the idioms that students tend to learn. Of course it depends on the idiom. There are many that we use a lot.

At the same time, it is clear that a lot of students like to learn idioms. A lot of intermediate level students have become tired of learning basic structures, or feel they know them, and grab at idioms as signs of tangible new things they can add to their knowledge. Idioms also can be a lot of fun.

Of course, it depends what we mean by an idiom. Every section of a unit in this book is full of idiomatic expressions, but the expressions in the 'Extra Expressions' section tend to be idiomatic phrases that can be isolated out as individual bits of knowledge. They are there for extra stimulation, and because no intermediate course is really complete without them. They will be appropriate for some classes but not for others, which is why they are on the 'Further Activities' page.

How to introduce them

First see if any of the students can make a sentence with one of the expressions. If they cannot, make some natural (and preferably humorous) sentences yourself until the students get the idea. They can then make their own sentences.

After going through each expression, put the students into pairs, and ask them to try and work out mini dialogues with each expression. There is an example dialogue in the book to help the students. When they have had time to do this, have sample pairs demonstrate their dialogues to the rest of the class.

The students should finish by writing down sample sentences or dialogues either on flip cards (see the 'Vocabulary' section) or in a special section of a file or note book.

6th page of a unit: Consolidation & Recycling

The activities in this section consolidate what has been learned in the rest of the unit and mix it with language from previous units. They can be used in class or done at home. Doing these activities will make a significant difference to how deeply the students retain words and structures.

It helps if the students do the written exercises except for the crossword on a computer or in a special notebook or file so they can keep a clear record of their progress. If they use computers, encourage them to use software that underlines mistakes or questionable grammar. This helps them reflect more on what they are writing.

BUILDING VOCABULARY

Just give the students the crosswords and see what happens. If you notice many students are having trouble with the same clue, give some hints or prompts to help.

Students can do the crosswords individually, in pairs or in groups. If they are not difficult for the students, it is better for them to be done individually. The answers to the clues come from the current unit or previous units.

FOCUSING ON COLLOCATIONS

The students put each pair of words into a separate sentence, preferably one that is meaningful. The collocation pairs in this section are from the current unit and the previous units.

Correcting written sentences

If a mistake is important, it is often better to indicate where the mistake is in the sentence by underlining the part that is wrong, and, if necessary, give some hint such as the starting word of a better pattern. This can be done in individual students' notebooks or on the board if you feel all the students will benefit from analyzing the mistake (it is not necessary to say which student made the mistake), and then ask students to suggest how to correct the mistake. This also applies when the students have not actually made a mistake but need to improve the style of a sentence.

Example:
Student's sentence:
Doing overtime has no connection with my tiredness.

The Stages of a Unit

Write   'There is ...' on the board.

This might elicit the sentence (maybe with your help):

> There is no connection between my tiredness and having to do overtime.

Cross out 'having' and write '... whether ...'. The aim is to elicit the sentence:

> There is no connection between my tiredness and whether I do overtime.

Avoid making any student feel bad by their sentence being analyzed and manipulated in this way. If possible, it is best to avoid making it obvious who made the mistake. It may also sometimes be better to change the original sentence a little or make a different model sentence that contains the same kind of mistake.

The students can then practice writing sentences that include the pattern you elicited.

WRITING OPINIONS

The students write paragraphs or short essays about each of the topics. Assign a minimum and maximum number of words, if necessary.

To make the activity more fun, students can be given points for including words and structures from a list that they manage to include in the paragraph. Some words/structures can be worth more points than others. You can identify words/structures they have been finding difficult and put them in the list.

If the students find paragraph writing difficult, it may be necessary to brainstorm ideas and arguments before they try and write. One way to do this is to get students to think of any ideas related to the topic and then extend these ideas through a kind of map—starting from one idea and drawing a line to another idea.

For example, you could write 'ideal friends' in a circle in the middle of the board or at the top of the board and ask the students to say anything they associate with this. They may say things like 'always kind', 'helping each other', 'having fun', 'travelling together' etc... You then write these down in circles leading off from the first circle. You then do the same for each of these patterns by asking, 'What do you connect with 'having fun?'. After a while, the students may begin to get ideas about how they could structure their essays.

Correction and rewriting

Correction can be done in the same way as in the 'Focusing On Collocations' section. It can also help a lot if the students rewrite their essays after becoming aware of their mistakes and of how they can improve the style.

REFLECTION

Encourage the students to answer the questions either in class or by writing their answers down and giving them to you. This can be very useful feedback. It is often a good idea to extend the list of questions, so that the students are filling in a short questionnaire at the end of each unit.

It also makes a big difference if the students reflect on the words and structures they found difficult in the unit, and write each of them on separate cards, perhaps with a sample sentence to show their usage. The students can build up this collection of cards and look through them as regularly as possible.

A Final Word

To provide a complete course for your students, you can help them widen their skills by encouraging the following:

Journals

The students keep a diary or notebook and write down anything they like in it. One idea is for students to keep this journal beside their bed, and for them to write down anything that occurs to them just before they sleep. They can write down what they have done that day, what they are thinking about ... in fact, anything they like.

Whether the students keep a journal, and whether they write or not should be up to them. We can actively encourage them to keep the journal, but it defeats the point if we make it obligatory. We also should not correct very much, if at all, unless a student obviously wants us to.

Extra reading

Encourage the students to read about anything they like. If they are interested in sport, they should read about sport. The more they enjoy what they read, the more reading they will do. They should not look up every word in a dictionary. They should read for content. To maximize the effectiveness of this approach, the level of the material is very important. Recommend graded readers or magazines if appropriate.

Extra listening

Encourage the students to watch TV or listen to English radio language-teaching programs if you think they are good and of the right level. You can also introduce them to tapes or listening courses they can use at home. Always be careful about level. Students can sometimes lose a lot of confidence and motivation by watching or listening to TV/radio shows that are too difficult, especially in an environment where they don't generally have much natural exposure to English in their daily lives.

An alternative, that often works very well, is to encourage students to bring small tape recorders to each lesson. They can then listen to the lesson again in their car, at home etc... This is particularly effective if the students don't have many lessons each week.

DEALING WITH MISTAKES

Don't worry too much about correcting mistakes in the early stages of a unit, though it is always good to make a note of these mistakes so you can deal with them later. In fact, it is best to build up a written list of key mistakes, and to address these problems systematically later in the same lesson or a subsequent lesson. Over a period of time, you can build up a list of the typical language points that your students have trouble with, and keep on coming back to these points.

At the moment the mistake is made, it can help a lot to correct the mistake in a natural way, and then move on without dwelling on the point.

Example:
Student: Almost of us still live with our parents.
Teacher: Really?! Almost all of you live with your parents. That's surprising!

In this case, the teacher has noticed that 'almost' is being used as a quantity instead of qualifying the quantity, but she does not explain this or make a big point of it. She introduces the correct use of 'almost' in a natural way, and makes a mental note of the problem. At a natural break, she writes down the problem in a book she keeps for this purpose, and comes back to the problem later in the lesson, like this:

Example:
Student: (reading) I like people that are sociable.
Teacher: How about you?
Student: Yes, I like people that are sociable, too.
Teacher: All people?
Student: Well ...
Teacher: (helps) Almost.
Student: ...almost all people that are sociable.

If the student makes the same mistake as before, the teacher again responds naturally:

Student: I like almost people that are sociable.
Teacher: Me, too. I like almost all people that are sociable, but not everybody. I don't like (e.g. famous TV personal-

The Stages of a Unit

ity that will cause students too smile or laugh). He's too sociable.

Other opportunities to introduce 'almost' come in the 'Personalization' and 'Focusing On Collocations' sections, where the teacher simply adds the structure 'Almost all ...' as a prompt for students to make sentences with. In fact, all key mistakes the students have made in the lesson, and some from previous lessons, can be added as prompts in these sections.

To be honest, a mistake such as the 'almost' problem above can be dealt with in almost any later section of the unit—during discussion, situational practice, written exercises etc...

Sections

1. Friends

POINTS OF VIEW: I like people that talk a lot.

Before listening or reading

A. Warm-up questions:

1. When do you feel bored?

_____

2. When do you feel comfortable?

_____

3. What kind of people do you like to hang out with?

_____

B. Anticipation gap-fill:

1. It's important for them to have a _____ of humor, too.

2. I prefer to have _____ who stand back and notice what's going on.

3. I might change my _____ if I have a serious relationship.

4. You'll probably start _____ for a lot of sensitive friends.

While listening or reading

Tomoko is the first speaker and Jin-Sook is the second speaker.

C. Listening/reading for gist:

1. Who do you think is more sociable, Tomoko or Jin-Sook?   _____

2. Who do you think is more serious, Tomoko or Jin-Sook?   _____

3. Who do you think is more sensitive, Tomoko or Jin-Sook?   _____

D. Noticing words: *(circle the words you hear/see)*

kind	deep	interested	anybody
sit	fed	in	reliable
shy	confident	sensitive	easily

E. Reading search:

1. How many words begin with 'c'?   _____

2. Find the opposite of 'interested'.   _____

3. Find something that means 'to date'.   _____

4. Find something that means 'tired of'.   _____

5. Find a word that is stronger than 'possibly'.   _____

After listening or reading

F. General questions:

1. What does Tomoko love having?

_____

2. What does Jin-Sook think of people that are sociable?

_____

3. Who does Tomoko want to hang out with?

_____

G. Correct these statements:

1. Tomoko loves having boring conversations.

_____

2. Jin-Sook prefers to have friends who sit down and look at the floor.

_____

3. Tomoko wants to hang out with friends that use air conditioners a lot.

_____

H. Comprehension/personalization questions:

1. What kind of people does Tomoko easily get bored with?

_____

2. What kind of people do you easily get bored with?

_____

3. What kind of people does Jin-Sook feel comfortable with?

_____

4. What kind of people do you feel comfortable with?

_____

5. What does Tomoko think is cool?

_____

6. What do you think is cool?

_____

2. Free Time

POINTS OF VIEW: I love being lazy!

Before listening or reading

A. Warm-up questions:

1. When are you lazy?

_____

2. What exercise do you take?

_____

3. How often do you go out with friends?

_____

B. Anticipation gap-fill:

1. I also like _____ walks.

2. I look _____ to it all day.

3. And there are so many other _____ to do.

4. I don't go to movies very _____.

While listening or reading

Michelle is the first speaker and Hassan is the second speaker.

C. Listening/reading for gist:

1. Who takes more exercise, Michelle or Hassan? _____

2. Who do you think goes out the most, Michelle or Hassan? _____

3. Who do you think has the most energy, Michelle or Hassan? _____

D. Noticing words: *(circle the words you hear/see)*

training	jogging	lunch	tennis
delicious	rowing	work	bad
easy	night	bowling	favorite

E. Reading search:

1. How many words begin with 'a'? _____

2. Find the opposite of 'stay home'. _____

3. Find something that means 'take it easy'. _____

4. Find a word that means less often than sometimes. _____

5. Find a word that is stronger than 'tired'. _____

After listening or reading

F. General questions:

1. What does Michelle think it's wonderful to do?

_____

2. How often does Michelle go out?

_____

3. How often does Hassan go to movies?

_____

G. Correct these statements:

1. Michelle likes taking photographs.

_____

2. Hassan goes for a swim in the bath.

_____

3. Hassan likes going fishing or hiking.

_____

H. Comprehension/personalization questions:

1. What does Michelle occasionally do?

_____

2. What do you occasionally do?

_____

3. What does Hassan look forward to all day?

_____

4. What do you look forward to all day?

_____

5. What does Michelle think is hard work?

_____

6. What do you think is hard work?

_____

3. The Past

POINTS OF VIEW: I played soccer all the time.

Before listening or reading

A. Warm-up questions:

1. What were you good at when you were younger?

_____

2. What is one of your happiest memories?

_____

3. What pets did you have when you were a child?

_____

B. Anticipation gap-fill:

1. I used to go and watch our local soccer _____.

2. The only thing he ever _____ about was soccer.

3. It sounds _____ you'll get skin cancer.

4. I spent most of my _____ with older people.

While listening or reading

Sonchai is the first speaker, Jin-Sook the second, Christina the third, and Carlos the fourth.

C. Listening/reading for gist:

1. Which of the four spent the most time indoors?   _____

2. Which of the four spent the most time with adults?   _____

3. Which of the four spent the most time at the beach?   _____

D. Noticing words: *(circle the words you hear/see)*

else	wonder	paintings	grow
date	fresh	prefer	sounds
remind	regret	playing	normally

E. Reading search:

1. How many words begin with 's'?   _____

2. Find the opposite of 'somebody'.   _____

3. Find something that means 'brown'.   _____

4. Find a word that goes with 'like' and 'as if'.   _____

5. Find a word that means 'usually'.   _____

After listening or reading

F. General questions:

1. What did Jin-Sook used to prefer doing?

_____

2. What did Christina take care of?

_____

3. Who did Carlos spend most of his time with?

_____

G. Correct these statements:

1. The only thing Jin-Sook's brother ever thought about was ice cream.

_____

2. Christina painted her pets.

_____

3. Carlos tells jokes all the time.

_____

H. Comprehension/personalization questions:

1. What sport did Sonchai play when he was a child?

_____

2. What sport did you play when you were a child?

_____

3. When could Jin-Sook swim?

_____

4. When could you swim?

_____

5. What does Christina think it's dangerous for children to do?

_____

6. What do you think it's dangerous for children to do?

_____

4. The Family

POINTS OF VIEW: We should live with elderly relatives.

Before listening or reading

A. Warm-up questions:

1. Who do you live with?

_____

2. How do your family help you?

_____

3. Do you think old people should live in special homes?

_____

B. Anticipation gap-fill:

1. It's our duty to look _____ our parents.

2. It's normal for children and their _____ to live in different cities.

3. We can often _____ a way to live with our parents.

4. The government should be _____ for taking care of old people.

While listening or reading

Hassan is the first speaker and Christina is the second speaker.

C. Listening/reading for gist:

1. Who thinks children should live with old parents? _____

2. Who thinks the family has changed a lot? _____

3. Who thinks the government should help more? _____

D. Noticing words: *(circle the words you hear/see)*

sacrifices	tax	usual	grandchildren
help	traditional	scattered	give
before	nowadays	expect	duty

E. Reading search:

1. How many words begin with 'e'? _____

2. Find another way to say 'take care of'. _____

3. Find the opposite of 'traditional'. _____

4. Find something that means 'can't avoid'. _____

5. Find a word that means 'to value'. _____

After listening or reading

F. General questions:

1. What would Hassan hate?

_____

2. What does Christina think is true?

_____

3. What does Christina suggest we should pay?

_____

G. Correct these statements:

1. Hassan thinks our parents made many jig-saw puzzles for us when we were children.

_____

2. Christina thinks some old people are shell fish.

_____

3. Christina suggests that homes for old people could be as exciting as possible.

_____

H. Comprehension/personalization questions:

1. What does Christina think is normal nowadays?

_____

2. What else do you think is normal nowadays?

_____

3. What does Hassan think we can find a way to do?

_____

4. What else do you think we can find a way to do?

_____

5. What does Christina think the government should be responsible for?

_____

6. What else do you think the government should be responsible for?

_____

5. Work

POINTS OF VIEW: In my ideal job, I'd have a lot of responsibility.

Before listening or reading

A. Warm-up questions:

1. How long are your vacations?

_____

2. How much time do you spend with your family?

_____

3. What gives an office a good atmosphere?

_____

B. Anticipation gap-fill:

1. I'd have many _____ to travel.

2. That kind of job wouldn't _____ me.

3. I think it would _____ on who your partner was.

4. I'd be happy with a _____ nine-to-five job.

While listening or reading

Lee is the first speaker and Sonchai is the second speaker.

C. Listening/reading for gist:

1. Who wants more responsibility?   _____

2. Who wants more time with his family?   _____

3. Who wants a less exciting job?   _____

D. Noticing words: *(circle the words you hear/see)*

enough	ambition	reasonable	overtime
manager	promoted	long	care
paperwork	meet	prefer	charge

E. Reading search:

1. How many words begin with 'r'?   _____

2. Find a word that means 'chances'.   _____

3. Find a word that goes with 'hours' and 'vacations'.   _____

4. Find something that means 'spend time together'.   _____

5. Find something that means 'on condition that'.   _____

After listening or reading

F. General questions:

1. What would Lee be prepared to do?

_____

2. Why does Lee think that not seeing your partner a lot might be good?

_____

3. What doesn't Sonchai care about?

_____

G. Correct these statements:

1. Lee would be able to start work late.

_____

2. Sonchai would be away from the office too much.

_____

3. Sonchai would be fine as long as he is a millionaire.

_____

H. Comprehension/personalization questions:

1. In his ideal job, what would Lee have many opportunities to do?

_____

2. In your ideal job, what would you have many opportunities to do?

_____

3. What would Sonchai like enough time to do?

_____

4. What would you like enough time to do?

_____

5. Who does Sonchai want to see a lot of?

_____

6. Who do you want to see a lot of?

_____

6. City Life

POINTS OF VIEW: Cities are noisy and polluted.

Before listening or reading

A. Warm-up questions:

1. Would/do you like to work in a large city? Why?

_____

2. Why do many young people want to live in cities?

_____

3. In which ways do large cities sometimes influence people's character?

_____

B. Anticipation gap-fill:

1. It sometimes takes hours to _____ to work.

2. Cities offer a chance to escape from a routine _____.

3. I feel _____ for people who go to big cities.

4. We need a chance to _____ city life.

While listening or reading

Carlos is the first speaker and Jin-Sook is the second speaker.

C. Listening/reading for gist:

1. Who prefers the country or small towns?   _____

2. Who thinks people in cities are mentally unhealthy? _____

3. Who thinks it's good to experience city life?   _____

D. Noticing words: *(circle the words you hear/see)*

suburb	drawn	glamorous	crowded
traffic	gym	stayed	materialistic
unfriendly	amenities	environment	gadgets

E. Reading search:

1. How many words begin with 'm'?   _____

2. Find the opposite of 'deep'.   _____

3. Find something that means 'decide'.   _____

4. Find a word that means 'most recent'. _____

5. Find a word that means 'steady'.   _____

After listening or reading

F. General questions:

1. Who does Carlos think are often unfriendly?

_____

2. Why does Carlos think people should stay in the country or small towns?

_____

3. What does Jin-Sook think we need a chance to do?

_____

G. Correct these statements:

1. It sometimes takes hours to wash the dishes.

_____

2. There aren't enough exciting opportunities in the kitchen.

_____

3. Carlos thinks discussing pop music is serious and deep.

_____

H. Comprehension/personalization questions:

1. What are there many more of in the cities than in country areas?

_____

2. What else are there many more of in the cities than in country areas?

_____

3. Who does Carlos feel sorry for?

_____

4. Who do you feel sorry for?

_____

5. What does Jin-Sook think we should make up our own minds about?

_____

6. What do you think we should make up our own minds about?

_____

7. Beliefs

POINTS OF VIEW: We can judge a person's character by their blood type.

Before listening or reading

A. Warm-up questions:

1. What are your ambitions?

_____

2. In which ways are you creative?

_____

3. What do you think of judging a person's character from their blood type?

_____

B. Anticipation gap-fill:

1. I've no _____ how it works.

2. I don't _____ a word of it.

3. Type B people stand _____ from the world around them.

4. I don't know why so many people are taken _____ by this kind of nonsense.

While listening or reading

Tomoko is the first speaker and Sonchai is the second speaker.

C. Listening/reading for gist:

1. Who is being cynical?   _____

2. Who believes in predictions from blood type?   _____

3. Who is talking about a friend?   _____

D. Noticing words: *(circle the words you hear/see)*

predict	teamwork	cynical	telepathy
sincere	true	conventional	unlucky
supposed	selfish	zodiac	interpret

E. Reading search:

1. How many words begin with 'c'?   _____

2. Find something that means 'invented'.   _____

3. Find something that means 'tricked'.   _____

4. Find two pairs of words that are opposites.   _____

5. Find something that means 'became rich'.   _____

F. General questions:

1. What is Sonchai's blood type?

_____

2. Which type are supposed to be creative?

_____

3. Who is the most conventional person Sonchai knows?

_____

G. Correct these statements:

1. Tomoko is considered very romantic in Japan.

_____

2. Type A people usually fight with others.

_____

3. Sonchai's friend has never eaten a thing in his life.

_____

H. Comprehension/personalization questions:

1. How does Tomoko compare with other people in Japan?

_____

2. How do you compare with other people in your country?

_____

3. What are type A people good at?

_____

4. What are you good at?

_____

5. What are many people taken in by?

_____

6. What are you taken in by?

_____

8. The Future

POINTS OF VIEW: Nobody will have to work.

Before listening or reading

A. Warm-up questions:

1. How do you think people will live 100 years from now?

_____

2. What problems might there be in the future?

_____

3. What will increase in the future?

_____

B. Anticipation gap-fill:

1. _____ anybody will have to work.

2. It could mean crime would _____.

3. We'll learn more about what _____ crime.

4. It sounds _____ we could lose control of our own lives.

While listening or reading

Christina is the first speaker and Manosh is the second speaker.

C. Listening/reading for gist:

1. Who thinks life will be more relaxing in the future?   _____

2. Who is more positive about the future?   _____

3. Who is more cynical?   _____

D. Noticing words: *(circle the words you hear/see)*

problems	invent	governed	wonder
materialism	unlikely	whatever	unless
doubt	discovered	enforce	fortune

E. Reading search:

1. How many words begin with 'p'?   _____

2. Find something that means 'it seems as if'.   _____

3. Find four things that may increase.   _____

4. Find something that means 'almost nobody'.   _____

5. Find two types of problems.   _____

After listening or reading

F. General questions:

1. What does Christina think we'll have much more of?

_____

2. If we get bored, what may happen?

_____

3. What does Christina think we'll learn more about?

_____

G. Correct these statements:

1. Scientists will discover how to keep people working hard.

_____

2. Everybody will be much hungrier than now.

_____

3. We could lose control of our animals.

_____

H. Comprehension/personalization questions:

1. What will happen if people live for hundreds of years?

_____

2. What will happen if you live for hundreds of years?

_____

3. What does Christina think there will be more time to do?

_____

4. What would you like more time to do?

_____

5. Who may be able to do whatever they like?

_____

6. If you could do whatever you like, what would you do?

_____

9. Transportation

POINTS OF VIEW: Driving is a good way to relax.

Before listening or reading

A. Warm-up questions:

1. How do you feel about driving?

_____

2. What things give you stress?

_____

3. Are cars good or bad for the environment?

_____

B. Anticipation gap-fill:

1. Driving is a good way to get _____ of stress.

2. I never drive to work any _____.

3. People that say driving is unhealthy don't know what they're _____ about.

4. Cars also _____ a lot of pollution.

While listening or reading

Tomoko is the first speaker and Karima is the second speaker.

C. Listening/reading for gist:

1. Who is negative about driving?   _____

2. Who likes to go to the countryside?   _____

3. Who is worried about the environment?   _____

D. Noticing words: *(circle the words you hear/see)*

breathe	fares	genuine	traffic
tax	public	punctual	stress
delayed	pollution	service	unhealthy

E. Reading search:

1. How many words begin with 's'?   _____

2. Find something that means 'remove'.   _____

3. Find a word that goes with 'ugly' and 'nicer'.   _____

4. Find something that means 'need too much'.   _____

5. Find a word that means 'prevent'.   _____

After listening or reading

F. General questions:

1. What effect does Karima think traffic jams have on people?

_____

2. What does Tomoko think it's fantastic to do?

_____

3. What does Karima think cars cause?

_____

G. Correct these statements:

1. Eating is one of the biggest causes of stress in our lives.

_____

2. It's much healthier to go by helicopter.

_____

3. Many people become too dependent on bananas.

_____

H. Comprehension/personalization questions:

1. How does Tomoko relax?

_____

2. How do you relax?

_____

3. What does Karima think many people don't do enough?

_____

4. What don't you do enough?

_____

5. What does Karima think there should be a higher tax on?

_____

6. What do you think there should be a higher tax on?

_____

10. Vices

POINTS OF VIEW: Smoking should be made illegal.

Before listening or reading

A. Warm-up questions:

1. Do you think smoking should be banned?

_____

2. Why don't governments ban smoking?

_____

3. If smoking is not banned, how should it be restricted?

_____

B. Anticipation gap-fill:

1. It's difficult for me to _____ why smoking is still legal.

2. We should be _____ to do a few things that are dangerous if we want to.

3. Millions of people are _____ of cancer unnecessarily.

4. It's reasonable to discourage pregnant _____ from smoking.

While listening or reading

Lee is the first speaker and Jin-Sook the second speaker.

C. Listening/reading for gist:

1. Who is in favor of smoking?   _____

2. Who is critical of the government?   _____

3. Who thinks smoking should sometimes be discouraged? _____

D. Noticing words: *(circle the words you hear/see)*

natural	drunk	legal	depressed
addicted	antisocial	income	passive
hangover	powerful	cancer	aware

E. Reading search:

1. How many words begin with 'a'?   _____

2. Find a word that's the opposite of 'legal'.   _____

3. Find a word that means 'strong'.   _____

4. Find a word that goes with 'sense', 'profit' and 'aware'.   _____

5. Find something that goes with 'natural', 'reasonable' and 'difficult'. _____

After listening or reading

F. General questions:

1. What does Jin-Sook think it's natural to do?

_____

2. Why does Lee think governments don't ban smoking?

_____

3. What does Jin-Sook think is unnecessary?

_____

G. Correct these statements:

1. Cigarettes are just as addictive as bananas.

_____

2. Governments shouldn't take all the English out of our lives.

_____

3. It's reasonable to have special areas for crocodiles.

_____

H. Comprehension/personalization questions:

1. What is it difficult for Lee to understand?

_____

2. What is it difficult for you to understand?

_____

3. What does Jin-Sook think we should be allowed to do if we want to?

_____

4. What do you think you should be allowed to do if you want to?

_____

5. What does Jin-Sook think it's reasonable to discourage?

_____

6. What do you think it's best to discourage?

_____

11. Marriage

POINTS OF VIEW: Weddings shouldn't be extravagant.

Before listening or reading

A. Warm-up questions:

1. How gorgeous do you think wedding ceremonies should be?

_____

2. Should wedding ceremonies be family gatherings?

_____

3. Should parents spend a lot of money when their children get married?

_____

B. Anticipation gap-fill:

1. In some countries people _____ ridiculous amounts of money.

2. It's not as crazy as it _____.

3. Their parents shouldn't _____ them by giving them so much.

4. Divorce is less _____ in countries with traditional marriage ceremonies.

While listening or reading

Christina is the first speaker and Tomoko is the second speaker.

C. Listening/reading for gist:

1. Who is in favor of traditional wedding ceremonies?   _____

2. Who is against expensive weddings?   _____

3. Who is trying to understand some parents' opinions?   _____

D. Noticing words: *(circle the words you hear/see)*

ceremony	propose	ridiculous	affair
impression	comfortably	arranged	single
engaged	divorce	appreciate	separate

E. Reading search:

1. How many words begin with 'c'?   _____

2. Find a word that is the opposite of 'modern'.   _____

3. Find something that means 'spent money'.   _____

4. Find a word that is the opposite of 'rare'.   _____

5. Find a word that goes with 'It's natural' and 'It's important'.   _____

After listening or reading

F. General questions:

1. Who does Tomoko think pays for new marriage expenses?

_____

2. What does Christina think happens when expensive things come too easily?

_____

3. What does Tomoko think the parents want the children to understand?

_____

G. Correct these statements:

1. Business meetings are special family gatherings.

_____

2. When expensive things come too cheaply, we don't like them.

_____

3. The parents want the couple to understand how important love is.

_____

H. Comprehension/personalization questions:

1. What do some people spend a lot of money on?

_____

2. What do you spend a lot of money on?

_____

3. What does Christina think it is important for married couples to do?

_____

4. What is it important for you to do?

_____

5. What does Tomoko think is less common in some countries than others?

_____

6. What do you think is less common in some countries than others?

_____

12. Animals

POINTS OF VIEW: There's no difference between eating cows and whales.

Before listening or reading

A. Warm-up questions:

1. How do you feel about eating meat?

_____

2. What's the difference between eating meat from a cow and from a whale?

_____

3. How do you feel about eating cats, dogs or horses?

_____

B. Anticipation gap-fill:

1. I realize that _____ customs vary a lot.

2. It's wrong to eat any animal that's in _____ of becoming extinct.

3. Some _____ of whales are not on the endangered list.

4. There are experiments that _____ that plants have feelings.

While listening or reading

Tomoko is the first speaker and Carlos is the second speaker.

C. Listening/reading for gist:

1. Who is against eating meat? _____

2. Who is in favor of eating some kinds of whales? _____

3. Who talks about experiments on plants? _____

D. Noticing words: *(circle the words you hear/see)*

morally	feelings	survival	evolution
reasonable	dying	endangered	wild
experiments	nature	reptiles	extinct

E. Reading search:

1. How many words begin with 'l'? _____

2. Find a word that means 'shocked'. _____

3. Find a word that means 'consideration' or 'point'. _____

4. Find a word that goes after 'accept' and 'realize'. _____

5. Find two words that add meaning to 'wrong'. _____

After listening or reading

F. General questions:

1. If we are not vegetarians, what does Tomoko think we should accept?

_____

2. What does Tomoko say about some kinds of whales?

_____

3. When would most of us be horrified?

_____

G. Correct these statements:

1. Many people get upset if we eat some vegetables but not others.

_____

2. Tomoko accepts that we shouldn't eat extinct species.

_____

3. There are experiments that show that teachers have feelings.

_____

H. Comprehension/personalization questions:

1. What does Tomoko think vary a lot?

_____

2. What do you think varies a lot?

_____

3. What does Carlos think is morally wrong?

_____

4. What do you think is morally wrong?

_____

5. What does Carlos think most people accept?

_____

6. What do you think most people accept?

_____

13. Computers

POINTS OF VIEW: Computer games are bad for children.

Before listening or reading

A. Warm-up questions:

1. What do you think is the most negative effect of computers on children?

_____

2. What do you think is the most positive effect of computers on children?

_____

3. How much did you use computers and watch TV when you were a child?

_____

B. Anticipation gap-fill:

1. I know children who play computer games all the _____.

2. Computer games can keep children's _____ for long periods of time.

3. Children need to run _____ and play with each other.

4. I expect they'll be pretty good at _____ all the new technology.

While listening or reading

Lee is the first speaker and Hassan is the second speaker.

C. Listening/reading for gist:

1. Who thinks computers are good for children?   _____

2. Who thinks children need to play outside more?   _____

3. Who thinks computers are better than TV?   _____

D. Noticing words: *(circle the words you hear/see)*

download	solving	access	unsociable
technology	virus	attachment	concentrate
delete	install	world	interactive

E. Reading search:

1. How many words begin with 's'?   _____

2. Find a word that goes with 'solving'.   _____

3. Find two things that mean 'also'.   _____

4. Find two words that follow 'must'.   _____

5. Find a word that means 'dealing with'.   _____

After listening or reading

F. General questions:

1. What abilities does Hassan think computers help?

_____

2. What does Lee think computers are bad for?

_____

3. What does Hassan think older people used to do instead of using computers?

_____

G. Correct these statements:

1. Lee knows children who are in a bed of their own.

_____

2. Lee thinks children shouldn't just sit in front of their mirrors.

_____

3. Hassan thinks their parents thought they'd become romantic and dangerous.

_____

H. Comprehension/personalization questions:

1. What does Lee think children don't know how to do?

_____

2. What do you think children don't know how to do?

_____

3. What does Lee think children need to do?

_____

4. What do you think children need to do?

_____

5. What does Hassan think children will be good at in the future?

_____

6. What do you think children will be good at in the future?

_____

14. The Generation Gap

Listening/Reading Worksheet

POINTS OF VIEW: Young people should get steady jobs.

Before listening or reading

A. Warm-up questions:

1. At what age should people try to find steady jobs?

_____

2. What kinds of jobs can creative and artistic people do?

_____

3. What kinds of people are often very conservative?

_____

B. Anticipation gap-fill:

1. Sooner or later you're going to have to find a good job and _____ down.

2. I get bored when I'm with people that want to be like everybody _____.

3. People like that are more effective in _____ society.

4. The managers don't listen to what we have to _____.

While listening or reading

Carlos is the first speaker and Karima is the second speaker.

C. Listening/reading for gist:

1. Who thinks it's best to have a normal job?   _____

2. Who thinks normal jobs are controlled by old people?   _____

3. Who thinks it's best to be part of the system?   _____

D. Noticing words: *(circle the words you hear/see)*

older	effective	immature	criticize
qualifications	fault	conforming	adolescent
follow	adult	argue	experience

E. Reading search:

1. How many words begin with 's'?   _____

2. Find something that means 'live a steady life'.   _____

3. Find four words that commonly collocate with 'get'.   _____

4. Find two ways to say 'do the same as others'.   _____

5. Find something that means 'there's no reason to'.   _____

F. General questions:

1. What kind of people does Karima want to be with?

_____

2. Who does Carlos think are effective in changing society?

_____

3. Why does Karima think there's no point in conforming?

_____

G. Correct these statements:

1. Karima thinks it's important for each of us to be somebody else.

_____

2. Carlos thinks there's no need to lose weight.

_____

3. Karima thinks when people get older they become more childish.

_____

H. Comprehension/personalization questions:

1. When does Karima get bored?

_____

2. When do you get bored?

_____

3. What do a lot of people try to improve?

_____

4. What do you try to improve?

_____

5. Who doesn't listen to what young people have to say?

_____

6. Who doesn't listen to what you have to say?

_____

15. Travel

POINTS OF VIEW: I usually join a tour group.

Before listening or reading

A. Warm-up questions:

1. What do you usually do when you have a vacation?

_____

2. What kinds of things do you like to do when you travel?

_____

3. How would you feel about taking an adventure holiday in the mountains or jungle?

_____

B. Anticipation gap-fill:

1. I usually join a tour group and we do everything _____.

2. When we travel we have to make an _____ to get to know local people.

3. I _____ if many people get long enough vacations.

4. They would be from various countries _____ of just from your own country.

While listening or reading

Christina is the first speaker and Sonchai is the second speaker.

C. Listening/reading for gist:

1. Who has shorter vacations?   _____

2. Who likes adventure?   _____

3. Who doesn't like tour groups?   _____

D. Noticing words: *(circle the words you hear/see)*

true	package	reasonable	insurance
confidence	exchange	abroad	galleries
share	lost	currency	countryside

E. Reading search:

1. How many words begin with 't'?   _____

2. Find something that means 'the same as'.   _____

3. Find a word that commonly collocates with 'away' and 'to know'.   _____

4. Find a word that commonly collocates with 'friends' and 'effort'.   _____

5. Find a word that commonly collocates with 'off', 'hiking' and 'cycling'.   _____

After listening or reading

F. General questions:

1. How does Christina usually travel?

_____

2. What kind of places does Sonchai like to visit?

_____

3. Why doesn't Christina think Sonchai is being reasonable?

_____

G. Correct these statements:

1. When Christina travels she can make a lot of new enemies.

_____

2. It's often said that travel broadens the stomach.

_____

3. There's a lot we can understand about agriculture from visiting museums.

_____

H. Comprehension/personalization questions:

1. What does Sonchai think we have to make an effort to do.

_____

2. What do you have to make an effort to do?

_____

3. What doesn't Christina have enough confidence to do?

_____

4. What don't you have enough confidence to do?

_____

5. What does Sonchai thing Christina won't want to go back to doing?

_____

6. What don't you want to go back to doing?

_____

1. Friends

A. Fill in the blanks with a possible word:

1. Witty people are good at _____ jokes.

2. We can depend on people who are _____.

3. She _____ being with a lot of people to being alone.

4. I feel _____ when I'm with people that are sensitive.

5. I'm _____ up with studying all the time.

6. We are very _____. We are both very easygoing.

7. I wish I _____, but I have to stay home.

8. If we spend time together, we'll be able to _____ our friendship.

9. I _____ into an old friend on the way here today.

10. I wish I could remember her name. It's on the _____ of my tongue.

B. Complete these sentences with your own ideas:

1. I can always depend on _____

2. I feel bored _____

3. I hardly talk to _____

4. I'm thinking of going _____

5. I couldn't have a deep relationship with _____

C. Quiz:

1. Name somebody on TV who is arrogant.   _____

2. Name a politician who is reliable.   _____

3. Name a fashion that is cool.   _____

4. Name an animal you think is selfish.   _____

5. Name a country that is very similar to your country.   _____

D. Jumbled up sentences:

1. wish jokes few tell she I would a.
   I _____

2. different they maybe so aren't.
   Maybe _____

3. mind married I if get change I my might.
   I _____

4. for looking girlfriend he'll start a probably.
   He'll _____

5. me very think between selfish you and I she's.
   Between _____

E. Sentences from words: *(write sentences that include these words)*

1. prefer

_____

2. hardly

_____

3. deep

_____

4. opposite

_____

5. friendship

_____

F. Writing dialogues: *(write at least an eight-line dialogue for each situation)*

1. Ask a friend out for dinner.

_____

_____

_____

_____

_____

_____

_____

2. Interview one of your best friends.

_____

_____

_____

_____

_____

_____

_____

1. Friends

3. You have just bumped into an old friend.

_____

_____

_____

_____

_____

_____

_____

_____

Unit Assessment

G. Word search:

N	D	S	E	L	F	I	S	H	L	A	M
V	S	L	A	Q	E	P	V	B	W	Y	U
A	E	R	S	N	D	S	L	M	U	X	E
O	R	Z	Y	G	F	C	O	T	D	M	S
P	I	R	G	N	D	E	V	E	L	O	P
P	O	J	O	X	P	V	E	U	N	Y	R
O	U	Y	I	G	K	T	R	M	Q	C	E
S	S	K	N	B	A	O	B	W	U	Y	F
I	B	E	G	X	C	N	O	T	I	C	E
T	R	Q	V	N	J	G	T	W	E	P	R
E	K	T	I	O	Z	U	W	I	T	T	Y
S	I	N	C	E	R	E	Y	R	Z	U	Q

There are 15 words from Unit 1 hidden in this puzzle.
Can you find them?
They are written either across, CAT,
down, C or diagonally, C.
A   A
T   T

_____   _____

_____   _____

_____   _____

_____   _____

_____   _____

_____   _____

_____   _____

_____

H. Hidden message:

1	2	3	4		5	6	7	–	8	9	9	10													
11	9	7	12		13	6	14	2			7	9		8	2	2	!		3	4	2		15	9	16
3	7	15	13	17	6	7	12		9	7		8	3	13	16	4	1	3	15		7	6	12	17	13
18	9	16	11	1			11	9	19	2			13	9			17	3	19	2		d	i	n	n
15	9	16			6		13	17	6	7	10		15	9	16		3	4	2		19	2	4	15	
3	7	1		10	6	7	1	,		3	7	1		6		18	9	16	11	1		11	9	19	2
1	2	19	2	11	9	21		9	16	4		22	4	6	2	7	1	8	17	6	21		14	9	4
15	9	16		18	6	11	11		8	3	15		15	2	8	.		20	3	4	11	9	8		

60 • Communication Strategies Teacher's Guide

2. Free Time

A. Fill in the blanks with a possible word:

1. I _____ to rush around doing a lot of things.

2. She just likes to _____ home.

3. It's _____ to lie on the sofa all day.

4. I can't _____ liking work more than free time.

5. If I was out of _____, I wouldn't be able to play tennis.

6. He can play the piano by _____.

7. I know how you _____.

8. I read a book on the train to _____ time.

9. We went on a _____ trip to New York and had a lot of meetings.

10. Just keep trying. _____ makes perfect.

B. Complete these sentences with your own ideas:

1. I would like more opportunities to _____

2. I rush around a lot _____

3. I'm sometimes too exhausted to _____

4. I wish I had more time to _____

5. I'm very fond of _____

C. Quiz:

1. Name a job that has many opportunities to travel.   _____

2. Name a movie star who is in very good shape.   _____

3. Name a restaurant that is often crowded.   _____

4. Name an animal you think is lazy.   _____

5. Name a country that has delicious food.   _____

D. Jumbled up sentences:

1. dog he of to take likes care his.

   He _____

2. that people understand I smoke can't.

   I _____

3. tired be she too to kind that must thing of do.

   She _____

4. not it she's may like married seem it but.

   It _____

5. easy stay I to take home it and like.

   I _____

2. Free Time

E. Sentences from words: *(write sentences that include these words)*

1. shape

_____

2. waste

_____

3. forward

_____

4. save

_____

5. practice

_____

F. Writing dialogues: *(write at least an eight-line dialogue for each situation)*

1. Order breakfast in a restaurant.

_____
_____
_____
_____
_____
_____
_____
_____

2. Interview a famous sportsman or sportswoman.

_____
_____
_____
_____
_____
_____
_____
_____
_____

3. Arrange a trip with a friend.

_____

_____

_____

_____

_____

_____

_____

_____

G. Word search:

G	Y	M	P	Y	E	N	E	R	G	Y	U
S	N	A	S	J	X	K	B	I	H	C	N
T	R	U	S	H	H	L	V	F	P	A	D
T	R	L	O	C	A	L	G	E	X	R	E
C	G	I	J	Q	U	P	W	E	N	E	R
R	V	C	P	Y	S	B	E	L	W	R	S
O	P	P	O	R	T	U	N	I	T	Y	T
W	U	F	Q	M	E	Z	O	N	P	G	A
D	Y	Z	T	X	D	K	F	G	Y	H	N
E	M	T	Z	H	J	U	T	C	W	L	D
D	E	X	T	R	E	M	E	L	Y	N	C
O	C	C	A	S	I	O	N	A	L	L	Y

There are 15 words from Unit 2 hidden in this puzzle.
Can you find them?
They are written either across, CAT,
down, C or diagonally, C.

A   A
T   T

_____   _____

_____   _____

_____   _____

_____   _____

_____   _____

_____   _____

_____

H. Hidden message:

1	2	3	4		5 C	3 a	4 r	6 l	7 o	8 s																						

3. The Past

Unit Assessment

A. Fill in the blanks with a possible word:

1. She doesn't easily _____ to new ways of doing things.
2. His parents didn't _____ him play very much.
3. We used to watch our _____ soccer team.
4. You _____ me of my father.
5. I took _____ of the flowers.
6. It seems like you didn't get a lot of _____ air.
7. Some people never really grow _____.
8. They all lived _____ ever after.
9. She enjoys being the center of _____.
10. I know my report is late, but better late than _____.

B. Complete these sentences with your own ideas:

1. I was brought up _____
2. I miss _____
3. I wonder if _____
4. It looks as if _____
5. I'd like to cut down on _____

C. Quiz:

1. Name a fashion that is out of date. _____
2. Name a famous person that likes to be the center of attention. _____
3. Name a local restaurant. _____
4. Name a country that used to be a superpower. _____
5. Name a custom that is traditional. _____

D. Jumbled up sentences:

1. fashions up I latest like with the keeping.
   I _____
2. local game watched whenever home we team had they our a.
   We _____
3. fresh didn't sounds like it air much you get.
   It _____
4. run house in buy have we'll to the a long.
   We'll _____
5. cut trying gambling down I'm smoking and to on.
   I'm _____

E. Sentences from words: *(write sentences that include these words)*

1. let

_____

2. memory

_____

3. seems

_____

4. normally

_____

5. true

_____

F. Writing dialogues: *(write at least an eight-line dialogue for each situation)*

1. Interview a famous person about his/her past.

_____

_____

_____

_____

_____

_____

_____

_____

2. Chat with a friend about a trip you took together.

_____

_____

_____

_____

_____

_____

_____

_____

3. The Past

3. Chat with a friend about memories of things you used to do together.

_____

_____

_____

_____

_____

_____

_____

_____

G. Word search:

M	T	H	E	M	S	E	L	V	E	S	C
P	R	J	F	K	R	E	G	R	E	T	K
R	A	E	B	G	V	N	R	Y	W	Q	Z
E	D	H	M	J	T	P	W	I	Z	J	M
F	I	G	R	I	W	M	E	M	O	R	Y
E	T	P	J	B	N	X	F	H	U	U	L
R	I	R	T	G	M	D	W	Q	T	S	S
W	O	N	D	E	R	J	P	H	S	E	C
T	N	L	N	V	B	V	Z	P	I	D	T
H	A	Z	S	E	E	M	S	K	D	R	R
E	L	S	E	W	V	A	G	U	E	Y	U
W	H	E	N	E	V	E	R	J	T	N	E

*There are 15 words from Unit 3 hidden in this puzzle.
Can you find them?
They are written either across, CAT,
down, C or diagonally, C.*

A   *A*
T   *T*

_____   _____

_____   _____

_____   _____

_____   _____

_____   _____

_____   _____

_____   _____

_____

H. Hidden message:

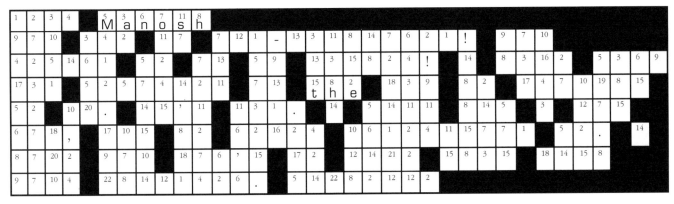

4. The Family

A. Fill in the blanks with a possible word:

1. He just wants to be free to be _____.

2. All her relatives are _____ all over the place.

3. She'd _____ it if she had to live by herself.

4. It may be _____ that I spend too much.

5. Am I _____ from a monkey?

6. What's the neighborhood _____?

7. My parents _____ me by giving me anything I wanted.

8. He doesn't have enough money to _____ his family.

9. I'm definitely the black _____ of my family.

10. Please come in and make _____ at home.

B. Complete these sentences with your own ideas:

1. I am criticized by _____

2. I can't stand _____

3. It's my duty to _____

4. It's true that _____

5. I take after _____

C. Quiz:

1. Name a famous person you think is spoiled. _____

2. Name somebody who has a lot of responsibility. _____

3. Name an animal that humans are descended from. _____

4. Name a very talented family. _____

5. Name somebody who works from home. _____

D. Jumbled up sentences:

1. wife does appreciate he his him things doesn't the for.
He _____

2. my elderly going will brother it's parents be after who my to look.
It's _____

3. government for helping people the should responsible be old.
The _____

4. children who selfish live old being to expect people with are their.
Old _____

5. department around there's corner just a store the.
There's _____

4. The Family

Unit Assessment

E. Sentences from words: *(write sentences that include these words)*

1. cousin

_____

2. sacrifice

_____

3. naughty

_____

4. unreasonable

_____

5. scattered

_____

F. Writing dialogues: *(write at least an eight-line dialogue for each situation)*

1. Interview a member of your family.

_____

_____

_____

_____

_____

_____

_____

_____

2. Talk at a real estate agency about an apartment you are interested in.

_____

_____

_____

_____

_____

_____

_____

_____

3. Criticize a member of your family.

_____

_____

_____

_____

_____

_____

_____

G. Word search:

A	P	P	R	E	C	I	A	T	E	C	X
J	P	A	R	E	N	T	S	M	C	O	P
D	N	Q	P	O	I	N	T	P	H	U	B
E	E	A	J	H	A	T	E	F	O	S	T
S	G	P	U	K	Z	F	Y	S	P	I	A
C	F	B	E	G	Z	R	W	U	J	N	L
E	A	Q	X	N	H	X	D	P	L	G	E
N	M	R	P	F	D	T	Z	P	Y	C	N
D	I	Q	E	K	N	B	Y	O	V	L	T
E	L	S	C	A	T	T	E	R	E	D	E
D	Y	F	T	Z	J	B	L	T	H	G	D
S	A	C	R	I	F	I	C	E	J	T	W

There are 15 words from Unit 4 hidden in this puzzle.
Can you find them?
They are written either across, CAT,
down, C or diagonally, C.
A   A
T   T

_____ _____

_____ _____

_____ _____

_____ _____

_____ _____

_____ _____

_____

H. Hidden message:

1	2	3	4		5 M	6 i	7 c	8 h	2 e	9 l	9 l	2 e														
10	11	12	4		13	11	14	2		15 w	3 a	16 s	12	13	4	2	3	16	11	13	3	17	9	2	.	6 , 5
16	12	4	2		10	11	12	4		18	3	14	8	2	4		5	3	1	2		5	3	13	10	
16	3	7	4	6	18	6	7	2	16		16	11		10	11	12		7	11	12	9	1		8	3	19	2
7	11	5	18	11	4	14	3	17	9	2		8	11	5	2		3	13	1		3		20	11	11	1
2	1	12	7	3	14	6	11	13	.		6		14	8	6	13	21		10	11	12		16	8	11
3	22	22	4	2	7	6	3	14	2		8	6	5		5	11	4	2	,		3	13	1		16	14
7	4	6	14	6	7	6	23	6	13	20		8	6	5		16	11		5	12	7	8	.	5	3	13

5. Work

A. Fill in the blanks with a possible word:

1. She was _____ to a higher position in her company.

2. Some of her _____ have become her best friends.

3. Having a steady job will be more secure in the long _____.

4. That kind of blouse doesn't _____ her.

5. Living separately would keep our relationship _____.

6. I don't _____ if I have a good job or not.

7. You might think _____ if you were married.

8. My office is very noisy so it's difficult to _____ on my work.

9. He showed up ten minutes _____.

10. Please tell me in _____ next time. I need time to prepare.

B. Complete these sentences with your own ideas:

1. My ambition is to _____

2. I'm prepared to _____

3. I'm fine as long as _____

4. I don't care if _____

5. I come home from work/school _____

C. Quiz:

1. Name a dynamic company.   _____

2. Name a job that is monotonous.   _____

3. Name a fashion that suits you.   _____

4. Name a store that has a nice atmosphere.   _____

5. Name a politician who you think is ambitious. _____

D. Jumbled up sentences:

1. together they fun lot a of have.
They _____

2. off danger being there's of laid always the.
There's _____

3. overtime be they'd of lot prepared do a to.
They'd _____

4. as job fine we'd reasonable as be had we a long.
We'd _____

5. differently if he woman was might a think he.
He _____

E. Sentences from words: *(write sentences that include these words)*

1. steady

_____

2. concentrate

_____

3. fresh

_____

4. self-employed

_____

5. qualifications

_____

F. Writing dialogues: *(write at least an eight-line dialogue for each situation)*

1. Interview a famous person about his/her ambitions.

_____

_____

_____

_____

_____

_____

_____

2. You are being interviewed for a job.

_____

_____

_____

_____

_____

_____

_____

5. Work

3. Telephone to say you cannot come to work/school.

_____

_____

_____

_____

_____

_____

_____

G. Word search:

O	K	H	Q	S	F	R	E	S	H	Z	J
V	M	O	N	O	T	O	N	O	U	S	N
E	T	U	G	R	Y	E	H	M	X	I	Z
R	F	R	P	R	E	P	A	R	E	D	T
T	J	S	P	F	K	Z	P	D	W	Q	N
I	L	L	Z	S	A	L	A	R	Y	J	N
M	A	N	A	G	E	R	P	H	G	W	F
E	I	M	Q	V	W	L	I	D	E	A	L
M	D	V	P	R	O	M	O	T	E	D	V
E	Z	P	A	P	E	R	W	O	R	K	T
E	X	C	I	T	E	M	E	N	T	A	L
T	R	U	C	W	Q	P	N	B	F	L	J

_There are 15 words from Unit 5 hidden in this puzzle.
Can you find them?
They are written either across, CAT,
down, C or diagonally, C._
         A   A
         T   T

_____   _____

_____   _____

_____   _____

_____   _____

_____   _____

_____   _____

_____   _____

_____

H. Hidden message:

1	2	3	4		5 H	3 a	6 s	6 s	3 a	7 n																
8	,	9	2		10	2	2	7		11	3	8	1		12	13	13	.		8	13		14	12 y	15 o u

6. City Life

A. Fill in the blanks with a possible word:

1. The bus is crowded so it's difficult to get a _____.

2. The _____ in some cities is terrible and often makes people sick.

3. The _____ around my house is very good. There's a large park nearby.

4. Because of the traffic jams, it often takes hours to _____ to work.

5. I want to escape from my _____ life and have more excitement.

6. It's dangerous to get _____ into that kind of world.

7. Is that _____ young people like to live in big cities?

8. I live in a _____ area. It's all houses and apartments.

9. The countryside is _____. There are no neon signs or vending machines.

10. We'll cross that _____ when we come to it.

B. Complete these sentences with your own ideas:

1. It can take a long time when _____

2. The only good thing I can say about _____

3. Cities offer a chance to _____

4. One of the most convenient areas _____

5. I sometimes get stuck _____

C. Quiz:

1. Name a city with a large population.   _____

2. Name a city that has good natural environment.   _____

3. Name a glamorous movie star.   _____

4. Name somebody you know who is materialistic.   _____

5. Name a famous farming area.   _____

D. Jumbled up sentences:

1. buildings here all made concrete around the of are.
   The

2. that lonely thing is surprising the feel I.
   The

3. gadgets they the time so electronic spend latest much discussing.
   They

4. off overslept and I my go didn't alarm.
   My

5. countryside the unspoiled surrounding very is.
   The

6. City Life

E. Sentences from words: *(write sentences that include these words)*

1. materialistic

_____

2. industrial

_____

3. amenities

_____

4. ridiculous

_____

5. environment

_____

F. Writing dialogues: *(write at least an eight-line dialogue for each situation)*

1. Plan a vacation with a friend.

_____
_____
_____
_____
_____
_____
_____
_____
_____

2. Chat with a friend about the area you live in.

_____
_____
_____
_____
_____
_____
_____
_____

3. Apologize to your boss/teacher for being late.

_____

_____

_____

_____

_____

_____

_____

G. Word search:

C	O	M	M	U	T	E	S	O	R	R	Y
H	P	E	Q	N	J	O	L	Y	R	Z	P
O	N	N	G	R	W	T	W	W	I	P	O
I	R	T	W	H	S	P	E	N	D	Q	P
C	Z	A	Q	T	R	A	F	F	I	C	U
E	F	L	S	L	K	X	T	K	C	G	L
K	H	L	H	U	N	W	Z	G	U	M	A
A	P	Y	A	F	B	C	K	V	L	G	T
R	Q	Y	L	Z	L	U	L	W	O	R	I
E	W	G	L	A	M	O	R	O	U	S	O
A	C	B	O	F	V	H	N	B	S	Y	N
C	R	O	W	D	E	D	S	T	U	C	K

There are 15 words from Unit 6 hidden in this puzzle. Can you find them?
They are written either across, CAT,
down, C or diagonally, C.
    A   *A*
    T   *T*

_____   _____

_____   _____

_____   _____

_____   _____

_____   _____

_____   _____

H. Hidden message:

7. Beliefs

A. Fill in the blanks with a possible word:

1. I could _____ what she said in many different ways.

2. It would stand a good _____ of becoming true.

3. I've _____ to believe in telepathy.

4. He's _____ very creative.

5. She doesn't believe a _____ of it.

6. She has no idea _____ it works.

7. It _____ have been your imagination.

8. I _____ believe in ghosts.

9. We are on the same _____ so we get along very well.

10. You look as if you've seen a _____.

B. Complete these sentences with your own ideas:

1. I predict that _____

2. Somebody probably made a lot of money _____

3. I don't know why _____

4. I deeply believe _____

5. Believe it or not, but _____

C. Quiz:

1. Name a famous superstition. _____

2. Name somebody who is cynical. _____

3. Name somebody who has predicted the future accurately. _____

4. Name somebody in the past who was very creative. _____

5. Name a religion many people believe in. _____

D. Jumbled up sentences:

1. predicted come he much of true what has.
Much _____

2. like I to what supposed am be?
What _____

3. salesman what I in by said taken was the.
I _____

4. answer sure the not what is I'm.
I'm _____

5. phenomena believe I supernatural genuinely in.
I _____

E. Sentences from words: *(write sentences that include these words)*

1. teller

_____

2. charm

_____

3. supposed

_____

4. cynical

_____

5. skeleton

_____

F. Writing dialogues: *(write at least an eight-line dialogue for each situation)*

1. Try to convince a friend that telepathy is possible.

_____

_____

_____

_____

_____

_____

_____

_____

2. Talk with a psychiatrist about a dream you have had.

_____

_____

_____

_____

_____

_____

_____

_____

7. Beliefs

3. Talk with somebody you have just fallen in love with (at first sight).

_____

_____

_____

_____

_____

_____

_____

G. Word search:

P	F	Q	A	S	T	R	O	L	O	G	Y
R	O	K	L	U	C	Y	N	I	C	A	L
E	R	W	R	P	T	W	V	Z	R	C	A
T	T	E	L	E	P	A	T	H	Y	L	R
T	U	Y	U	R	W	R	Q	J	B	O	O
Y	N	N	C	N	N	X	E	L	B	S	U
Z	E	J	K	A	F	G	W	D	Q	E	N
P	O	F	Y	T	Y	P	E	J	I	T	D
I	G	D	B	U	T	P	W	F	M	C	L
W	K	Z	I	R	D	E	E	P	L	Y	T
R	C	R	E	A	T	I	V	E	V	Z	G
C	P	H	H	L	C	S	T	R	O	K	E

There are 15 words from Unit 7 hidden in this puzzle.
Can you find them?
They are written either across, CAT,
down, C or diagonally, C.
A   A
T   T

_____   _____

_____   _____

_____   _____

_____   _____

_____   _____

_____   _____

_____   _____

_____

H. Hidden message:

1	2	3	4		5	2	2																					
6	7	8		9	7	8	10	1		9	7		11 c	6 y	10 n	12 i	11 c	3 a	5 l	!		12		13	14	12	10	15
13	14	2	4	2	,	9		3		5	7	13		7	16		13	4	8	13	14		12	10		13	14	12	10	17	9
5	12	15	2		18	8	1	17	12	10	17		7	8	4		11	14	3	4	3	11	13	2	4		16	4	7	19		7	8	4
20	5	7	7	1		13	6	21	2		3	10	1		21	4	2	1	12	11	13	12	10	17		13	14	2
16	8	13	8	4	2		16	4	7	19		7	8	4		22	2	1	12	3	11		5	9	12	17	10	.		12		3	5	9	7
1	2	2	21	5		20	2	5	12	2	23	2		12	10		23	3	19	21	12	4	2	9	,		17	14	7	13	9
3	10	1		13	2	5	2	21	3	13	14	6	.		11	14	4	12	9	13	12	10	3						

8. The Future

A. Fill in the blanks with a possible word:

1. I _____ what our lives will be like in the future.

2. She invented a new kind of computer that _____ her a fortune.

3. It won't happen _____ my luck changes.

4. If _____ anybody works, there'll be a terrible population problem.

5. We'll be able to _____ crime more effectively.

6. It might _____ I wouldn't have to work.

7. Don't _____ up hope!

8. My dream of going to Hawaii came _____.

9. Don't count your chickens before they're _____ .

10. You never _____ what's going to happen.

B. Complete these sentences with your own ideas:

1. Nobody knows _____

2. I doubt _____

3. We'll learn more about what causes _____

4. I have a future plan to _____

5. The only hope I have of _____

C. Quiz:

1. Name a science fiction movie.   _____

2. Name a bad crime.   _____

3. Name a problem that may get worse in the future. _____

4. Name the person who invented the electric light. _____

5. Name the person who discovered penicillin.   _____

D. Jumbled up sentences:

1. family try my support earn to money I'll to enough.
   I'll _____

2. luck had she amazing of an stroke.
   She _____

3. problems lead might to that of lot social a.
   That _____

4. manager hope up of gave becoming he a.
   He _____

5. next know will week never happen you what.
   You _____

8. The Future

E. Sentences from words: *(write sentences that include these words)*

1. unless

_____

2. cause

_____

3. unlikely

_____

4. guess

_____

5. slight

_____

F. Writing dialogues: *(write at least an eight-line dialogue for each situation)*

1. Talk with a friend about future plans.

_____

_____

_____

_____

_____

_____

_____

2. Talk to a time traveler from the future.

_____

_____

_____

_____

_____

_____

_____

_____

3. Ask somebody to marry you.

_____

_____

_____

_____

_____

_____

_____

G. Word search:

S	C	I	E	N	T	I	S	T	S	Y	K
J	R	T	F	H	J	U	N	L	E	S	S
D	I	S	C	O	V	E	R	V	Y	K	F
Q	M	X	Z	L	W	G	M	Q	E	M	F
T	E	P	J	N	B	Z	W	B	L	N	U
Q	K	X	N	G	J	D	P	C	H	W	T
J	N	Z	P	U	N	O	B	O	D	Y	U
B	K	W	L	E	Y	U	L	U	K	A	R
F	N	R	F	S	C	B	B	N	M	L	E
W	O	R	K	S	G	T	Q	T	V	I	X
H	W	K	J	B	M	G	N	T	B	V	Z
C	S	L	I	G	H	T	Z	G	C	E	W

There are 15 words from Unit 8 hidden in this puzzle. Can you find them?
They are written either across, CAT,
down, C or diagonally, C.

A   A
T   T

_____   _____

_____   _____

_____   _____

_____   _____

_____   _____

_____   _____

_____   _____

H. Hidden message:

1	2	3	4		5	6	4	7	8	9	7	10	3															
10 N	11 o	12 b	11 o	1 d	13 y		5	3	10		14	4	2	1	7	5	9		9	6	2		15	16	9	16	4	2			3	10	1
7		1	11	16	12	9		7	15		8	16	14	2	4	10	3	9	16	4	3	17		9	6	7	10	18	8
2	19	7	8	9		.		18	6	11	8	9	8		3	10	1		20	3	21	14	7	4	2	8		6	3	20	2
12	2	2	10		7	10	20	2	10	9	2	1		12	13		8	16	14	2	4	8	9	7	9	7	11	16	8
14	2	11	14	17	2		.		7		2	19	14	2	5	9		9	6	3	9		7	10		9	6	2		15	16	9	16	4	2
8	5	7	2	10	5	2		22	7	17	17		14	4	11	20	2		9	3	6	9		9	6	2	13		3	4	2
23	16	8	9		7	21	3	18	7	10	3	9	7	11	10	.		17	2	2

9. Transportation

Unit Assessment

A. Fill in the blanks with a possible word:

1. Once you get a computer, you'll always be _____ on it.

2. My car often breaks _____.

3. It's easy to _____ around on a bicycle.

4. Getting _____ in traffic jams makes people irritated.

5. I'm _____ about drives in the countryside.

6. You can't _____ me that smoking is healthy.

7. The traffic _____ changed to red.

8. If you don't hurry, you'll _____ the train.

9. I don't know the _____ thing about engines.

10. It's easy when you know _____.

B. Complete these sentences with your own ideas:

1. I'm thinking of getting _____

2. I don't know why _____

3. It's fantastic to _____

4. Cars make _____

5. The traffic is often heavy _____

C. Quiz:

1. Name somebody who isn't punctual.   _____

2. Name something that causes pollution.   _____

3. Name something that spoils the countryside.   _____

4. Name somebody who is dependent on a car.   _____

5. Name a convenient type of public transportation.   _____

D. Jumbled up sentences:

1. to car when I use have only a I.
   I _____

2. here punctual very the not transportation around public is.
   The _____

3. stress rid good walking of way is to a get.
   Walking _____

4. ugly signs countryside neon the make.
   Neon _____

5. talking know she what about doesn't she's.
   She _____

E. Sentences from words: *(write sentences that include these words)*

1. uncomfortable

_____

2. irritated

_____

3. pollution

_____

4. congested

_____

5. nonsense

_____

F. Writing dialogues: *(write at least an eight-line dialogue for each situation)*

1. Talk with a friend about local transportation.

_____

_____

_____

_____

_____

_____

_____

_____

2. Talk to a rich person about why he/she has a submarine.

_____

_____

_____

_____

_____

_____

_____

_____

9. Transportation

3. Persuade a police officer that you were not driving dangerously.

_____

_____

_____

_____

_____

_____

_____

Unit Assessment

G. Word search:

P	U	N	C	T	U	A	L	Q	F	G	D
U	J	O	H	B	A	M	V	W	L	G	E
B	C	N	Y	D	E	L	A	Y	E	D	P
L	O	S	B	R	E	A	K	R	K	J	E
I	N	E	C	A	T	C	H	I	M	G	N
C	V	N	X	R	W	F	Q	H	N	H	D
F	I	S	K	P	G	Z	A	Q	P	G	E
N	N	E	L	G	R	W	C	R	K	L	N
B	C	C	O	N	G	E	S	T	E	D	T
Q	E	T	V	M	I	S	S	N	H	S	J
S	E	R	V	I	C	E	R	S	P	J	H
I	R	R	I	T	A	T	E	D	W	Q	F

There are 15 words from Unit 9 hidden in this puzzle.
Can you find them?
They are written either across, CAT,
down, C or diagonally, C.
_A   A_
_T   T_

_____   _____

_____   _____

_____   _____

_____   _____

_____   _____

_____   _____

_____

H. Hidden message:

1	2	3	4		5	3	4	6	7	3																				
8	9	10		1	9	11	,	12		5	11	9	13		13	14	3	12		8	9	10	,	4	2		12	3	15	5	6	11	16
3	17	9	10	12	!		6	18		12	14	2	4	2	,	19		3		14	6	16	14	2	4		12	3	20		9	11
21	3	4	19	,		7	9	4	2		22	2	9	22	15	2		13	6	15	15		10	19	2								
10	11	21	9	7	18	9	4	12	3	17	15	2		3	11	1		21	4	9	13	1	2	1		22	10	17	15	6	21
12	4	3	11	19	22	9	4	12	3	12	6	9	11	.		3	11	1		6	18		12	14	2		17	10	19	2	19
3	11	1		12	4	3	6	11	19		17	2	21	9	7	2		7	9	4	2		22	9	22	10	15	3	4	,	12	14	2
18	3	4	2	19		13	6	15	15		6	11	21	4	2	3	19	2	.		14	3	19	19	3	11				

10. Vices

A. Fill in the blanks with a possible word:

1. _____ they get is a hangover the next day.

2. She tried to _____ up smoking once.

3. Many people who drink too much _____ up as alcoholics.

4. It doesn't make _____ to ban marijuana but not smoking.

5. Governments get a lot of money from the _____ on cigarettes.

6. I don't understand why you think there's some big _____.

7. She makes it a _____ to come to school very early.

8. I avoid places that sell ice cream so as to keep away from _____.

9. I'd be very _____ if you could help me.

10. Do you _____ if I open the window?

B. Complete these sentences with your own ideas:

1. I'm thinking of giving up _____

2. I don't have the willpower to _____

3. It's difficult to understand why _____

4. I should be allowed to _____

5. I wish I could find a way to _____

C. Quiz:

1. Name somebody who's addicted to TV.   _____

2. Name something that causes heart attacks.   _____

3. Name a company that makes a profit.   _____

4. Name something illegal.   _____

5. Name a popular form of gambling.   _____

D. Jumbled up sentences:

1. stop people when to some know talking don't.
   Some _____

2. unnecessarily people heart of dying are of attacks millions.
   Millions _____

3. drinking discourage from reasonable from it's to alcoholics.
   It's _____

4. this have long like been how feeling you ?
   How _____

5. dinner pyjamas my if lunch you cook in do I?
   Do _____

10. Vices

Unit Assessment

E. Sentences from words: *(write sentences that include these words)*

1. cancer

_____

2. depressed

_____

3. pregnant

_____

4. habit

_____

5. gamble

_____

F. Writing dialogues: *(write at least an eight-line dialogue for each situation)*

1. Talk with a friend about something you want to give up.

_____

_____

_____

_____

_____

_____

_____

_____

2. Ask somebody not to smoke in your home.

_____

_____

_____

_____

_____

_____

_____

_____

3. You are sick. Talk about the problem with a doctor.

_____

_____

_____

_____

_____

_____

_____

_____

G. Word search:

W	I	L	L	P	O	W	E	R	M	Z	A
P	F	Q	E	J	A	T	T	A	C	K	N
R	R	H	L	G	G	R	W	X	C	V	N
E	P	O	B	N	A	T	U	R	A	L	O
G	A	N	F	M	K	L	W	P	N	H	Y
N	I	G	M	I	J	K	V	B	C	R	I
A	D	D	I	C	T	E	D	T	E	Q	N
N	W	F	N	L	P	N	F	W	R	Z	G
T	J	K	D	Q	P	A	S	S	I	V	E
Z	A	N	T	I	S	O	C	I	A	L	G
H	B	D	I	S	C	O	U	R	A	G	E
T	E	M	P	T	A	T	I	O	N	H	X

There are 15 words from Unit 10 hidden in this puzzle. Can you find them?
They are written either across, CAT,
down, C or diagonally, C.
    A   *A*
    T   *T*

_____   _____

_____   _____

_____   _____

_____   _____

_____   _____

_____   _____

_____   _____

_____

H. Hidden message:

11. Marriage

Unit Assessment

A. Fill in the blanks with a possible word:

1. I don't have many chances to meet members of the _____ sex.

2. Don't traditional marriages have high _____ rates?

3. In love marriages, one of the couple may have _____ expectations.

4. Some people spend _____ amounts of money on their honeymoons.

5. It's _____ for parents to want children to be as happy as possible.

6. It's important for new couples to build their homes _____ by themselves.

7. He loves her with all his _____.

8. He's my _____ husband. We're getting married next month.

9. He often comes home late at night, so his wife has become very _____.

10. We were going out together but we've just _____ up.

B. Complete these sentences with your own ideas:

1. It's important for _____

2. I don't appreciate _____

3. My impression is that _____

4. My guess is that _____

5. If he/she marries me, I'll _____

C. Quiz:

1. Name somebody who had a white wedding.   _____

2. Name somebody who's extravagant.   _____

3. Name a famous person you'd like to get to know. _____

4. Name somebody who's engaged.   _____

5. Name a country that has many arranged marriages. _____

D. Jumbled up sentences:

1. arranged soon will couples if marriages separate the are.

   If _____

2. money people clothes ridiculous on spend of amounts some new.

   Some _____

3. appreciate comes when too love don't easily it we.

   When _____

4. seems job as as new seems is finding it a not easy.

   Finding _____

5. together up go but we we to split used out.

   We _____

E. Sentences from words: (*write sentences that include these words*)

1. single

_____

2. propose

_____

3. ridiculous

_____

4. faithful

_____

5. common

_____

F. Writing dialogues: (*write at least an eight-line dialogue for each situation*)

1. Plan a wedding ceremony with your future husband/wife.

_____
_____
_____
_____
_____
_____
_____
_____

2. Talk with a friend about what to give somebody as a wedding present.

_____
_____
_____
_____
_____
_____
_____
_____

11. Marriage

3. We are on holiday together. Argue with me about what to do.

_____
_____
_____
_____
_____
_____
_____
_____

G. Word search:

A	N	N	I	V	E	R	S	A	R	Y	F
C	F	I	M	P	R	E	S	S	I	O	N
E	Q	F	S	I	N	G	L	E	D	F	C
R	J	M	A	K	L	F	B	Q	I	W	S
E	S	P	L	I	T	H	A	X	C	Y	E
M	R	B	Q	K	R	Z	P	L	U	W	E
O	R	O	M	A	N	T	I	C	L	B	M
N	F	H	O	N	E	Y	M	O	O	N	S
Y	S	E	P	A	R	A	T	E	U	K	L
J	H	A	G	J	M	W	Z	N	S	N	W
N	F	R	G	R	A	D	U	A	L	L	Y
E	X	T	R	A	V	A	G	A	N	T	X

_There are 15 words from Unit 11 hidden in this puzzle.
Can you find them?
They are written either across, CAT,
down, C or diagonally, C._

A   A
T   T

_____   _____
_____   _____
_____   _____
_____   _____
_____   _____
_____   _____
_____   _____
_____

H. Hidden message:

12. Animals

A. Fill in the blanks with a possible word:

1. It's _____ to eat animals on the endangered list.

2. _____ of the fittest seems to be a law of nature.

3. Many species are _____ out.

4. _____ of looking at things vary a lot.

5. There is no _____ between eating horses and eating sheep.

6. It's wrong to eat any animal that's in _____ of becoming extinct.

7. Most people _____ that we need to eat meat to survive.

8. She dresses up very nicely and likes to _____ for compliments.

9. When the cat's _____ the mice will play.

10. It must be true. I got it _____ from the horse's mouth.

B. Complete these sentences with your own ideas:

1. I'm not sure whether _____

2. The way things are going _____

3. I realize that _____

4. I think it's morally wrong to _____

5. I would be horrified if _____

C. Quiz:

1. Name a domestic animal.   _____

2. Name a carnivorous animal.   _____

3. Name an extinct animal.   _____

4. Name an endangered animal.   _____

5. Name somebody who behaves like an animal. _____

D. Jumbled up sentences:

1. animal wrong of extinct it's eat danger to any becoming in that's.
It's _____

2. be money factor sure I'm whether deciding the not should.
I'm _____

3. fish split sea but we've there up the more in plenty are.
We've _____

4. worm bird early the catches the.
The _____

5. relatives mouse be when as as had stayed quiet my with we we to a.
When _____

12. Animals

Unit Assessment

E. Sentences from words: *(write sentences that include these words)*

1. wild

_____

2. tame

_____

3. pain

_____

4. particularly

_____

5. factor

_____

F. Writing dialogues: *(write at least an eight-line dialogue for each situation)*

1. Chat with a friend at the zoo.

_____
_____
_____
_____
_____
_____
_____
_____
_____

2. Talk with a friend about becoming a vegetarian.

_____
_____
_____
_____
_____
_____
_____
_____

3. Buy an unusual pet in a pet shop.

_____

_____

_____

_____

_____

_____

_____

_____

G. Word search:

D	G	E	N	D	A	N	G	E	R	E	D
N	J	X	R	W	D	Y	A	X	Z	C	M
A	T	P	E	V	O	L	U	T	I	O	N
D	K	E	G	H	M	R	Q	I	U	H	L
M	Y	R	M	B	E	F	S	N	J	R	H
I	S	I	Q	V	S	C	T	C	H	Q	E
T	P	M	N	X	T	Z	R	T	A	M	E
F	E	E	K	G	I	R	A	P	B	A	Z
R	C	N	H	N	C	B	I	Z	G	M	F
F	I	T	T	E	S	T	G	W	V	M	J
R	E	Y	W	Q	V	Z	H	A	W	A	Y
F	S	U	G	G	E	S	T	E	D	L	B

There are 15 words from Unit 12 hidden in this puzzle.
Can you find them?
They are written either across, CAT,
down, C or diagonally, C.
    A   *A*
    T   *T*

_____   _____

_____   _____

_____   _____

_____   _____

_____   _____

_____   _____

_____

H. Hidden message:

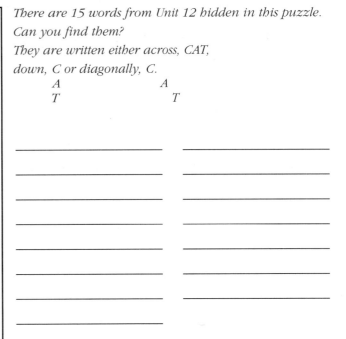

13. Computers

A. Fill in the blanks with a possible word:

1. My computer was infected by a _____.

2. You can _____ the software from the Internet.

3. Many people may try and get _____ to my computer.

4. Many children are in a _____ of their own.

5. Computers can keep children's _____ for long periods of time.

6. I hate to _____ what these children will be like when they grow up.

7. They'll be more _____ about new technology.

8. It _____ be good to go to bed so late every night.

9. I _____ e-mail a few times a day and always find many messages.

10. She doesn't really love me. It was just _____ thinking.

B. Complete these sentences with your own ideas:

1. I send e-mails _____

2. I can install _____

3. I can't easily relate to _____

4. I hate to think _____

5. I'm good at handling _____

C. Quiz:

1. Name an interactive computer game. _____

2. Name some useful software. _____

3. Name a computer company that sounds like a fruit. _____

4. Name something that's bad for our eyesight. _____

5. Name something that keeps children's attention. _____

D. Jumbled up sentences:

1. problem software she's that caused the the deleted.
   She's _____

2. software downloading anti-virus worth it's.
   It's _____

3. people children relate many to to how know other don't.
   Many _____

4. things games ability working computer children's to help at keep.
   Computer _____

5. around curious what's children going them very are about on.
   Children _____

E. Sentences from words: *(write sentences that include these words)*

1. attachment

_____

2. on-line

_____

3. screen

_____

4. information

_____

5. latest

_____

F. Writing dialogues: *(write at least an eight-line dialogue for each situation)*

1. Chat with a friend about your favorite computer games.

_____

_____

_____

_____

_____

_____

_____

_____

2. Discuss the importance of computers.

_____

_____

_____

_____

_____

_____

_____

_____

13. Computers

3. Buy a computer in a store.

_____

_____

_____

_____

_____

_____

_____

_____

G. Word search:

P	B	A	V	S	N	E	X	P	E	C	T
V	U	T	G	C	H	E	C	K	L	H	D
I	N	T	E	R	A	C	T	I	V	E	U
R	S	A	Y	E	A	Q	N	W	F	C	L
U	O	C	B	E	C	P	W	V	O	K	L
S	C	H	F	N	C	V	H	Z	L	R	W
J	I	M	K	S	E	B	J	I	G	R	K
W	A	E	M	U	S	T	Q	N	C	B	F
J	B	N	X	R	S	L	W	K	W	S	J
B	L	T	E	C	H	N	O	L	O	G	Y
G	E	N	E	R	A	T	I	O	N	X	C
D	O	W	N	L	O	A	D	K	L	V	B

There are 15 words from Unit 13 hidden in this puzzle.
Can you find them?
They are written either across, CAT,
down, C or diagonally, C.
  _A_   _A_
  _T_   _T_

_____   _____

_____   _____

_____   _____

_____   _____

_____   _____

_____   _____

_____   _____

_____

H. Hidden message:

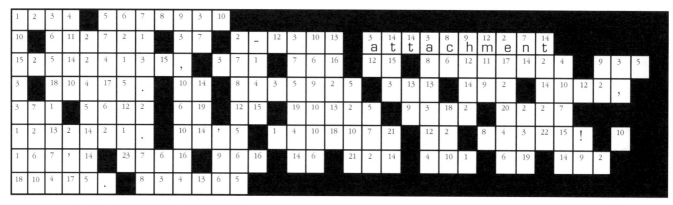

14. The Generation Gap

A. Fill in the blanks with a possible word:

1. They treat us as if we were immature _____.

2. Her parents find _____ in almost everything she does.

3. My opinions just _____ to be different from theirs.

4. We have a _____ to live our own lives.

5. It's important for each of us to be _____.

6. They are _____ gaining the experience to improve things.

7. There's no _____ in conforming.

8. I thought she was twenty. She doesn't look her _____.

9. The younger _____ these days only think about fashion.

10. He can't make up his mind. He just sits on the _____.

B. Complete these sentences with your own ideas:

1. I sometimes argue with _____

2. I'm sometimes criticized by _____

3. I don't think there's any point in _____

4. There's no need to _____

5. It doesn't get me anywhere when I _____

C. Quiz:

1. Name somebody who often criticizes others.　　_____

2. Name somebody who doesn't look their age.　　_____

3. Name somebody who doesn't act their age.　　_____

4. Name a conservative politician.　　_____

5. Name a radical politician.　　_____

D. Jumbled up sentences:

1. her why criticize she people understands older.
She _____

2. qualifications get later some I'll sooner have or to.
Sooner _____

3. changes gradually I'm power gaining the make to.
I'm _____

4. anywhere job us getting get doesn't steady a.
Getting _____

5. wall her banging like mind trying brick a to head my change against is.
Trying _____

14. The Generation Gap

E. Sentences from words: *(write sentences that include these words)*

1. settle

_____

2. generation

_____

3. mature

_____

4. gradually

_____

5. fault

_____

F. Writing dialogues: *(write at least an eight-line dialogue for each situation)*

1. Chat with a friend about the attitudes of older people.

_____

_____

_____

_____

_____

_____

_____

_____

2. Chat with a friend about the attitudes of younger people.

_____

_____

_____

_____

_____

_____

_____

_____

Unit Assessment

3. Discuss with an older person how life was different 30-40 years ago.

_____

_____

_____

_____

_____

_____

_____

_____

G. Word search:

C	O	N	F	O	R	M	P	G	K	L	N
O	R	E	A	S	O	N	Q	O	J	M	I
N	E	Y	U	S	K	H	M	P	W	Q	M
S	B	P	L	E	A	W	A	G	Z	E	P
E	E	M	T	T	V	D	T	K	J	M	R
R	L	G	R	T	G	Q	U	N	F	A	O
V	X	W	B	L	J	Z	R	L	Q	G	V
A	D	O	L	E	S	C	E	N	T	A	E
T	O	U	R	S	E	L	V	E	S	Z	P
I	R	A	D	I	C	A	L	K	W	I	R
V	H	J	W	R	G	Q	Z	B	F	N	Z
E	X	P	E	R	I	E	N	C	E	E	F

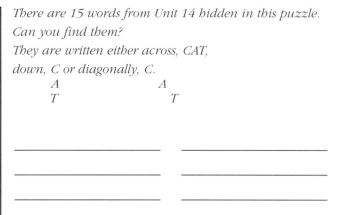

There are 15 words from Unit 14 hidden in this puzzle.
Can you find them?
They are written either across, CAT,
down, C or diagonally, C.
    A   *A*
    T   *T*

_____ _____

_____ _____

_____ _____

_____ _____

_____ _____

_____ _____

_____ _____

_____

H. Hidden message:

15. Travel

Unit Assessment

A. Fill in the blanks with a possible word:

1. I can get a _____ ticket from a travel agency.

2. I don't think there's any danger so I don't take out any _____.

3. She prefers to go away for a few days just to change her _____.

4. We don't get long enough vacations to do that kind of _____.

5. I don't have enough confidence to go on my _____.

6. I _____ that once you get away, you'll never want to go back.

7. Paris is a very popular tourist _____.

8. I was late and _____ the flight.

9. We went to a country area to get some peace and _____.

10. When I went to Hawaii I had the time of my _____.

B. Complete these sentences with your own ideas:

1. I sometimes get lost _____

2. I know a nice out-of-the-way place _____

3. I doubt if _____

4. I guess _____

5. I'd like to share _____

C. Quiz:

1. Name a famous tourist sight in Europe.   _____

2. Name somebody who likes sunbathing.   _____

3. Name somebody who isn't reasonable.   _____

4. Name a strong currency.   _____

5. Name an important type of insurance.   _____

D. Jumbled up sentences:

1. rate vacation cost the the the on exchange of depends.
   The _____

2. flight long jet lag after usually a I get.
   I _____

3. mind say the that travel people broadens.
   People _____

4. ticket get doubt discount a I if to able I'll be.
   I _____

5. vacation quiet when away I I peace get take just get to some a like and and.
   When _____

E. Sentences from words: *(write sentences that include these words)*

1. souvenirs

_____

2. local

_____

3. bet

_____

4. adventure

_____

5. annual

_____

F. Writing dialogues: *(write at least an eight-line dialogue for each situation)*

1. Buy a ticket at a travel agency.

_____

_____

_____

_____

_____

_____

_____

_____

2. Recommend what a visitor should do in your country.

_____

_____

_____

_____

_____

_____

_____

_____

15. Travel

3. Talk with a local person when you are on vacation.

_____

_____

_____

_____

_____

_____

_____

Unit Assessment

G. Word search:

```
S U N B A T H E T C W P
O M J D M B Q K B O H A
U T I I O T R I P N G C
V O K S J U W O Q F Y K
E U L C S F B F A I Z A
N R L O C A L T P D Q G
I N S U R A N C E E H E
R Q W N C Y C L I N G X
S X C T F G R T P C L K
Z E X C H A N G E E M N
D E S T I N A T I O N G
```

There are 15 words from Unit 15 hidden in this puzzle. Can you find them?
They are written either across, CAT,
down, C or diagonally, C.
  A   A
  T   T

_____   _____

_____   _____

_____   _____

_____   _____

_____   _____

_____

H. Hidden message:

1	2	3	4		5	6	7	-	8	9	9	10																								

(In the fourth row, cells under a set of boxes spell: **b e a u t i f u l**)

Page 102

Oral Interview Questions

Unit 1

1. Talk about the kind of people you like.

2. Talk about the kind of people you do not like.

3. Talk about somebody you are similar to.

4. Talk about a friend of the family.

5. Imagine you are telephoning me. Ask me out for dinner.

Unit 2

1. Talk about what you do in your free time.

2. Talk about how much exercise you take.

3. Talk about the times you waste time.

4. Talk about things you don't have time to do.

5. Imagine you are at a restaurant. Order dinner.

Unit 3

1. Talk about things you enjoyed doing when you were a child.

2. Talk about your memories of your family life when you were a child.

3. Talk about your memories of school when you were a child.

4. Talk about things you regret about the past.

5. Tell a fairy story you know.

Unit 4

1. Talk about your family.

2. Describe your ideal family life.

3. Describe your ideal house.

4. How much should parents control children?

5. How should children help parents when they are old?

Unit 5

1. Talk about your ideal job.

2. Talk about whether you want responsibility at work.

3. Talk about about the good points and bad points of a regular office job.

4. Talk about whether it's good to be self-employed.

5. You are being interviewed by me for a job of your choice.

Oral Interview Questions

Unit 6

1. Compare living in the city with living in the countryside.

2. Talk about a famous or beautiful place in your area.

3. Imagine you are giving a guided tour of your area.

4. Talk about another city or area you like.

5. Apologize to me for being late for work.

Unit 7

1. Talk about your blood type and whether it suits your character.

2. Talk about whether you believe in ghosts.

3. Talk about love at first sight.

4. Talk about what you think is lucky and unlucky.

5. Try to convince me that ghosts exist.

Unit 8

1. Talk about your hopes and dreams.

2. Guess what will happen to your country in the future.

3. Guess what will happen to the world in the future.

4. Talk about what you will be able to do when you can speak English fluently.

5. Persuade me to give you a million dollars.

Unit 9

1. Talk about the good points and bad points of cars.

2. Talk about the best ways to get around the city/area you live in.

3. Talk about how transportation may develop in the future.

4. Talk about the healthiest ways to travel.

5. I'm a policeman and I've stopped you for speeding. Argue with me.

Unit 10

1. Talk about the reasons people smoke.

2. Talk about the reasons why smoking is not banned.

3. Talk about your vices.

4. Talk about whether you gamble and why or why not.

5. I'm a doctor. Imagine you are sick. Discuss your problem with me.

Unit 11

1. Talk about the good points and bad points of being married.

2. Talk about arranged marriages.

3. Talk about your ideal husband/wife.

4. Talk about whether love can last forever.

5. I'm a wedding planner. Talk with me about the wedding ceremony you would like.

Unit 12

1. Talk about the good points and bad points of having a pet.

2. Talk about the animal you like most.

3. Talk about vegetarianism.

4. Talk about how we can prevent animals from becoming extinct.

5. I work in a pet shop. Buy a pet from me.

Unit 13

1. Talk about how computers have changed people's lives.

2. Talk about the effect of computers on children.

3. Talk about how you think computers will develop in the future.

4. Talk about the good points and bad points of e-mail.

5. I work in a computer store. Buy a computer from me.

Unit 14

1. Talk about how things have changed since your parents' generation.

2. Talk about whether young people should get normal jobs.

3. Talk about how to change society.

4. Talk about the best age to be.

5. I'm much older than you. You think the world is much better than it was. Argue with me.

Unit 15

1. Talk about an interesting place you have visited.

2. Talk about how you like to travel.

3. Talk about the place you'd most like to visit.

4. Talk about the best ways to get to know other people when you travel.

5. I'm visiting your area. Recommend places for me to visit.

1. Friends

Tomoko: Carlos has no sense of *humor*. He's always so *serious*. I wish he would tell a few jokes sometimes.

Jin-Sook: He's just not very *sociable/witty/confident*, and not very *sociable/witty/confident* either. I think he just prefers being by himself. I really like him, though. I just wish he was a bit more *confident* in social situations, and he's too *sensitive* so he gets hurt easily.

Tomoko: I must admit, he's a great guy! He's a very *reliable* friend, so I can always depend on him in a crisis. Even when I'm extremely *arrogant/selfish* and *arrogant/selfish*, he doesn't seem to mind at all.

2. Free Time

Lee: I don't have much free time, and I tend to *rush around* doing a lot of things. I don't like to *waste* time.

Christina: I'm very different. I work very hard, too, so when I have free time I feel *exhausted* and just want to stay home. I like to *take care of* my pets and plants. They really help me *calm down* and feel relaxed.

Lee: I'm *fond of* pets, too, but I prefer using my free time actively to staying at home. I often *eat out* at nice restaurants, and use every *opportunity* I have to *take a trip/eat out* somewhere.

3. The Past

Manosh: I guess I'm *old-fashioned/out of date/traditional*. I was *brought up* in a very *traditional/old-fashioned* family, and I don't easily adapt to new ways of doing things.

Tomoko: It sounds like you don't have much fun! When I was a child I always *used to/had to* study, and my parents *didn't let* me play in the evenings, so now I just like having fun and keeping up with the latest fashions. As soon as something's *out of date*, I'm not interested in it any more.

Manosh: You *remind me of* my sister. She's just like you! I think you'll *regret* it later, and wish you had been more interested in culture and history and not just in temporary fashions.

4. The Family

Michelle: I can't live at home. My parents *criticize/depend on* me almost all the time. It may sound like I don't *appreciate* everything they've done for me, but I just want to be free to be myself. Besides, my older sister and her husband are at home and I can't stand my brother-*in-law*.

Karima: I don't live at home either, but for different reasons. My parents used to *spoil/look after* me so much. They would give me almost anything I wanted, and *sacrifice* what they wanted, so that I would be happy. I left home because I didn't want to *depend on/criticize* them any more.

Michelle: My sister and her husband are going to live in Hawaii, and all my *cousins* and other *relatives* are scattered all over the place, so I think it's going to be me who will *look after* my parents when they get older. I wonder if I'll have the strength to be a good daughter.

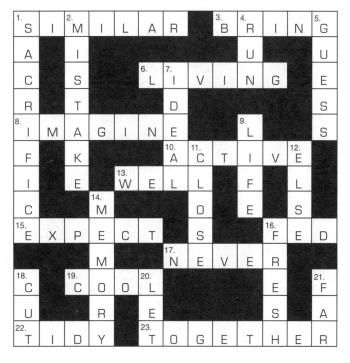

5. Work

Hassan: I was *promoted/laid off* last month, so now I'm a *manager/civil servant*. I'm *in charge of* the office computer system.

Karima: So you work in an office? I couldn't do that! I'm sure I'd hate working for a large corporation or being a *civil servant*. I need more *excitement* in my life.

Michelle: Having a *steady/monotonous* office job is not so bad. It's not just *paperwork*. A lot of my colleagues have become my best friends, and we have a lot of fun together. Though, to be honest, my *ambition* is to have my own business. I think being *self-employed* will be more secure in the long run. When working for a large corporation, there's always the danger of being *laid off*.

6. City Life

Christina: I live in the *suburb* of a large city. If I'm lucky it only takes twenty minutes to *commute* to work, but when there's a *traffic jam* it can take up to two hours! So I go by train, but it's often difficult to get a seat because the train is so *crowded*.

Manosh: I live in a city, too, and the *environment* around my house is not very good. Everything's made of concrete! And there are hardly any trees. But the local *amenities* are good. There are a lot of good shops, and there's a gym nearby.

Christina: The only good thing I can say about the city is that it's good for my work. The surprising thing about living in the city is that even though it has such a large *population*, and there are many *stimulating/ glamorous* things to do, I feel much lonelier than I did when I lived in a small town.

7. Beliefs

Carlos: I went to see a *fortune teller* a few years ago, and she was able to *predict* many things about my future. It's amazing that so much of what she said has come true.

Michelle: She probably said things that you could *interpret* in many different ways. So whatever she said would stand a good chance of coming true.

Carlos: You're being too *cynical*. I'm sure she was genuine. Since then I've become very interested in studying the stars, so I read a lot about *astrology* and the *zodiac*. And I've also come to believe in *supernatural* phenomena such as *vampires/ghosts* and *vampires/ghosts*.

Crossword solution grid:

1.S	U	R	R	2.O	U	N	D	I	N	3.G	4.G
U				U		O				5.A	G	E
P		6.S	T	A	N	D				V	
E	7.B		S		S		8.W	H	E	N	
9.R	O	U	T	I	N	E	A			10.C
S		I		D		11.N	E	V	E	12.R	O
13.T	E	L	L	E	R	S		E		O	N
I		D					14.L	O	O	K	S
T			15.W			E		M			I
16.I	N	L	A	W		17.M	I	N	D		D
O			S			E		G		18.O	E
19.N	E	X	T			N		T		20.F	O	R
			21.E	N	O	U	G	H		F	S

8. The Future

Lee: I *wonder* what we will all be doing ten years from now. I *doubt/wonder* if I'll be living a very exciting life. I'll *probably* be married and trying to earn enough money to support my family.

Hassan: *Nobody knows* what's going to happen. The future is so *unpredictable*. You might *invent/discover* something that will make you a fortune. You could be a millionaire *by the time* you are forty!

Lee: Not *unless* I have an amazing stroke of luck! It's very *unlikely* that anything like that will happen. I *guess* I'll just be doing a normal nine-to-five job.

Crossword solution grid:

1.P	R	2.O	B	3.L	E	M		4.H	U	5.M	O	6.R
R		F		O						A		E
7.E	F	F	E	C	8.T	I	V	E	L	Y		M
D		I		A		D				9.M	E
I		10.C	O	L	L	E	A	G	11.U	E	M
C		E		A					N		B
12.T	13.O		14.S	L			15.L	O	S	E
	T		O		16.R	17.M	I		E	R
18.H	O	U	S	E	W	O	R	K	E	
	E		N		L	D		E		19.A
20.G	R	21.A	D	U	A	T	E	L		W
		I			X	R		22.Y	E	A	R
	23.T	R	I	P		N			Y	

9. Transportation

Sonchai: I'm thinking of getting a car. It will be much easier to *get around*. The *public transportation* around here is not very reliable. The trains are often *delayed* because of the weather, and the buses aren't very *punctual*.

Manosh: Yes, I don't know why the bus *service* is so bad. The *fares* are very high, too, and the seats are often *uncomfortable*. But cars have problems as well. They sometimes *break down*, and once you get one, you'll always be *dependent on* it.

Sonchai: I'll just use it when I have to, and when the roads are not too *congested*. I won't use it all the time.

1.A	C	C	U	R	A	T	E		5.I	D	E	6.A
C		O		O	R							T
7.C	O	M	M	U	T	E		8.F				T
I		F		T	9.A	P	P	L	Y			E
D		O		I	T			Y				N
E		10.R	I	N	G		11.M	I	G	H	T	
N		T		E		12.W	N				I	
13.T	E	A	M		14.B	E	I	N	G		O	
	B		15.S		S				16.T	17.A	N	
18.T	E	L	E	P	A	T	H	Y		B		
E	E		A		H			20.F	R	O	M	
L			A		E			O		V		
21.L	E	A	V	E		22.M	A	R	R	I	E	D

10. Vices

Karima: I can't stand people that get *drunk*. Some people don't know when to stop drinking, and they think they are so clever and their opinions are so wonderful! All they get is a *hangover* the next day.

Carlos: I tried to *give up* drinking once, and I almost succeeded. I'd become *addicted* to alcohol, and was scared of having a *heart attack*. Unfortunately, I lacked the *willpower* to completely stop.

Karima: I can understand people drinking too much when they are very *depressed* or having a lot of stress, but it's so unpleasant for other people around them. And a lot of people who drink too much end up as *alcoholics*.

1.P	A	S	S	I	V	E		E		5.B	E	D	6.D
O		K		I				N		E			R
7.W	H	E	T	H	E	R		8.V	A	G	U	E	
E		L		W				I		I			A
R		E				9.R	U	N		I			M
F		10.T	O	B	A	C	C	O		N			S
U		O				Y		N		E			
12.L	O	N	G	13.G		N		14.M	O	R	E	15.E	
				A		16.T	17.I	M	E			A	
18.P	A	I	D			19.C	E	N	T	E	R		
A				G		A		T				N	
20.I	L	L	E	G	A	L						E	
N				T				21.M	I	N	D		

11. Marriage

Manosh: In my country, there are still a lot of marriages *arranged* between families. Even these days this can be a very good system for people that are shy or that don't have many chances to *get to know* members of the *opposite sex*.

Michelle: I can understand how that system may have worked well in the past, but I think, nowadays, many young couples will soon *separate/divorce* if their partners are decided by their families. Don't these kinds of marriages have high *divorce* rates?

Manosh: I doubt it. I know it's more romantic to think we should *propose* to the one we love, get *engaged*, then married, and live happily ever after. But, don't you think in love marriages, one or the other of the couple has unrealistic expectations, becomes disappointed, and may even be having an *affair* before the second or third wedding *anniversary*! I think I'll stay *single*!

12. Animals

Christina: Many *wild* animals are now *dying out/ extinct/endangered*. The way things are going, there will be very few larger animals in the world except *domestic* ones like cows or sheep. It's very unnatural.

Lee: Maybe it's very natural! *Survival of the fittest/Evolution* is a basic law of *nature/evolution*, and Man has come out on top. We are the fittest! The other *mammals*, and all the insects and *reptiles* are simply not as good at surviving as we are.

Christina: That's a very cruel opinion. Many *species/mammals* are *dying out/extinct/endangered* and you just think it's natural! I suppose if aliens invade the earth and make Man *extinct*, that will also be natural.

13. Computers

Manosh: Somebody sent me an *attachment/virus* the other day and it infected my computer. I've *deleted* the file that caused the problem and it didn't do too much damage, but I think I'd better *install* some anti-*virus* software.

Sonchai: It's easy to do. You can *download* the software from the Internet or use a *CD-ROM*. It's also worth improving the general *security* of your computer, especially if it is part of a *network* or if it is permanently *on-line*. You don't need to worry so much if you dial up using a *modem*, but that's much less convenient.

Manosh: Yes. I've heard all kinds of people may try and get *access* to my computer if I'm not careful. I don't know why! I don't keep anything important on it.

1. A	C	C	E	S	2. S		3. S		4. D	5. E	L	6. E	T	E
T			O		E				X			A		
7. T	A	M	E		8. C	U	L	T	U	R	E		9. C	
A			M		R			I		L			C	
10. C	H	O	I	11. C	E			N		12. Y	O	U	R	
H			N	13. A	T	T	A	C	K				I	
M				L				T					O	
E		14. S	I	15. M	P	L	Y		16. T				S	
N		E		R				17. A	R	E	A	S		
18. T	E	C	H	N	O	L	O	G	Y				I	
		U		O					E		19. M		T	
		R		I						20. A	N	Y		
21. V	E	G	E	T	A	R	I	A	N					

14. The Generation Gap

Jin-Sook: Why is it that older people are so often more *conservative* than younger people? And why do so many older people treat us as if we were *immature* children?

Michelle: I know what you mean. My parents *find fault* in almost everything I do, so we always *argue*. They completely misunderstand me. I'm not a *rebel/radical*. I'm not even an *adolescent* any more. I'm a mature *adult* with my own opinions, that just happen to be different from theirs.

Jin-Sook: Our ideas may sometimes seem too *radical*, so I understand why older people *criticize* us, but we have a right to live our own lives and make our own mistakes. I know they do it because they love us, but ...

1. G	E	N	U	I	N	2. E		3. N		4. A	5. S		6. I
E						E		A			7. M	E	A	N
N				8. S	T	O	9. P			A			T
E					U		A			L		10. M	E
R					R		11. R	U	12. L	E			R
13. A	N	Y	14. W	H	E	R	E		V			A
T			O			N		E		C
15. I	N	16. F	O	R	M	A	T	17. I	O	N		T
O		A		S			N		E		I
N		18. C	R	E	A	T	19. I	V	E		V
		T		B			E		20. O	W	E
		O		L			N		N
21. A	R	G	U	E		22. S	T	R	E	S	S

15. Travel

Michelle: I go *abroad* a lot, and it doesn't usually cost very much. I can get a *discount ticket* from the *travel agency*, I don't stay in expensive hotels, I don't buy many *souvenirs*, and each trip is short so I don't take out any *insurance*. Of course, the total cost depends on the *exchange rate*. If the local *currency* is strong, it can be very expensive.

Hassan: I don't like to travel so much, and I always suffer from *jet lag* for the first few days, so if I go anywhere, I like to take long trips, and usually to *out-of-the-way* places.

Michelle: I'd *get lost* if I went to places like that, and I prefer to take short trips just to change my feeling. I often go to an island for a few days and just *sunbathe* on the beach.

1.D	E	2.S	T	I	N	3.A	T	I	O	5.N		6.U
I		I				R		N		E		P
7.V	A	M	P	I	R	E		9.S	E	E	M	S
O		I		N		A		U		D		E
10.R	E	L	A	T	E		R		11.S	I	T	
C		A		E		12.E	X	A	M			
E		13.R	E	L	A	X		N		15.T		14.S
				L		C		C				I
16.W				I		17.E	V	E	N	I	N	G
18.O	F	19.F		G		P				C		H
R		I		E		20.T	H	I	N	K		T
21.L	I	V	I	N	22.G					E		S
D		E		23.T	O	U	R	I	S	T		

Teacher's Book Answers

The students may come up with alternative answers that are also possible. These should be encouraged and accepted.

UNIT 1

Listening/reading worksheet

B
1. sense   2. friends   3. mind
4. looking

D
kind, deep, anybody, fed, shy, sensitive, easily

E
1. 6: conversations, comfortable, couldn't, close, cool, change
2. bored
3. go out with
4. fed up with
5. probably

F
1. She loves having lively, witty conversations with friends.
2. She thinks they are often arrogant.
3. She wants to hang out with friends that are cool.

G
1. She loves having lively, witty conversations.
2. She prefers to have friends who stand back and notice what's going on around them.
3. She wants to hang out with friends that are cool.

H
1. She easily gets bored with people who are quiet or shy.
3. She feels comfortable when she's with people who are quiet.
5. She thinks it's cool to be a bit arrogant.

Unit assessment

A
1. telling   2. reliable   3. prefers

4. bored   5. fed   6. similar
7. could   8. develop   9. bumped
10. tip

D
1. I wish she would tell a few jokes.
2. Maybe they aren't so different.
3. I might change my mind if I get married.
4. He'll probably start looking for a girlfriend.
5. Between you and me, I think she's very selfish.

G
Word search
selfish, serious, arrogant, easygoing, fed, bump, love, develop, tongue, quiet, notice, witty, prefer, sincere, opposite

H
Hidden message
Dear Jin-Sook,
Long time no see! Are you doing anything on Saturday night? I would love to have dinner with you. I think you are very sincere and kind, and I would love to develop our friendship more. I hope you will say yes. Carlos.

UNIT 2

Listening/reading worksheet

B
1. taking   2. forward   3. things
4. often

D
training, tennis, delicious, work, night, bowling

E
1. 9: all, also, and, a, after, aerobics, are, almost, as
2. go out
3. relax
4. occasionally
5. exhausted

F

1. She thinks it's wonderful to lie on the beach all day/relax in front of the TV watching one of her favorite videos.
2. She goes out almost every night.
3. He doesn't go very often.

G

1. She likes taking walks (or lying on the beach etc…).
2. He goes for a swim in the pool.
3. He likes going dancing or bowling (or doing weight training etc…).

H

1. She occasionally plays tennis or golf.
3. He looks forward to going to the gym (or doing weight training etc…).
5. She thinks going to the gym (or doing weight training etc…) is hard work.

Unit assessment

A

1. tend	2. stay	3. wonderful
4. imagine	5. shape	6. ear
7. feel	8. kill	9. business
10. practice		

D

1. He likes to take care of his dog.
2. I can't understand people that smoke.
3. She must be too tired to do that kind of thing.
4. It may not seem like it, but she's married.
5. I like to stay home and take it easy.

G

Word search

exhausted, opportunity, shape, occasionally, feeling, energy, understand, extremely, crowded, local, rush, often, trip, gym, care

H

Hidden message

Dear Carlos,
Tomoko and I are going to the gym on Saturday.

We both feel out of shape and need to do some exercise. We could all eat out and go to a movie in the evening if you like, but hope we won't be too exhausted. Jin-Sook.

UNIT 3

Listening/reading worksheet

B

1. team	2. thought	3. like
4. time		

D

else, wonder, grow, fresh, prefer, sounds, remind, playing, normally

E

1. 10: soccer, so, swim, surf, sounds, skin, spend, spent, seems, serious
2. nobody
3. tan
4. sounds
5. normally

F

1. She used to prefer going to the beach.
2. She took care of her pets.
3. He spent most of his time with older people.

G

1. The only thing he thought about was soccer.
2. She painted pictures.
3. He's a serious person.

H

1. He played soccer.
3. She could swim when she was four.
5. She thinks it's dangerous for children to spend much time outside.

Unit assessment

A

1. adapt	2. let	3. local
4. remind	5. care	6. fresh

Teacher's Book Answers

7. up   8. happily   9. attention
10. never

D

1. I like keeping up with the latest fashions.
2. We watched our local team whenever they had a home game.
3. It sounds like you didn't get much fresh air.
4. We'll have to buy a house in the long run.
5. I'm trying to cut down on gambling and smoking.

G

Word search
traditional, whenever, remind, else, themselves, serious, wonder, used, outside, regret, memory, prefer, seems, true, vague

H

Hidden message
Dear Manosh,
You are so old-fashioned! You remind me of my father! I have many bad memories of the way he brought me up. It's sad. I miss him a lot now, but he never understood me. I hope you won't be like that with your children. Michelle.

UNIT 4

Listening/reading worksheet

B

1. after   2. parents   3. find
4. responsible

D

sacrifices, tax, scattered, nowadays, expect, duty

E

1. 3: even, expect, enough
2. look after
3. modern
4. can't help
5. appreciate

F

1. He'd hate it if his grandparents had to live by themselves or in a special home for old people.
2. She thinks it's true that we owe our parents a lot.
3. She suggests we should pay more tax.

G

1. He thinks they made many sacrifices for us.
2. She thinks some old people are selfish.
3. She suggests that they could be as nice as possible.

H

1. She thinks it's normal for children and their parents to live in different cities.
3. He thinks we can often find a way to live with our parents after they become old.
5. She thinks they should be responsible for taking care of old people.

Unit assessment

A

1. himself   2. scattered   3. hate
4. true   5. descended   6. like
7. spoiled   8. support   9. sheep
10. yourself

D

1. He doesn't appreciate the things his wife does for him.
2. It's going to be my brother who will look after my elderly parents.
3. The government should be responsible for helping old people.
4. Old people who expect to live with their children are being selfish.
5. There's a department store just around the corner.

G

Word search
descended, appreciate, depend, sacrifice, spoil, expect, scattered, parents, talented, support, naughty, family, cousin, hate, point

H

Hidden message

Dear Michelle

Your note was unreasonable. I'm sure your father made many sacrifices so you could have a comfortable home and a good education. I think you should appreciate him more, and stop criticizing him so much. Manosh.

UNIT 5

Listening/reading worksheet

B

1. opportunities   2. suit   3. depend
4. steady

D

enough, reasonable, overtime, long, care, meet, prefer

E

1. 3: responsibility, relationship, reasonable
2. opportunities
3. long
4. see a lot of each other
5. as long as

F

1. He'd be prepared to do a lot of overtime.
2. He thinks it might keep the relationship fresh.
3. He doesn't care if he has responsibility or not.

G

1. He'd be able to take long vacations.
2. He'd be away from home too much.
3. He'd be fine as long as he has a reasonable salary.

H

1. He'd have many opportunities to travel and meet interesting people.
3. He'd like enough time to build a happy home.
5. He'd like to see a lot of his children.

Unit assessment

A

1. promoted   2. colleagues   3. run
4. suit   5. fresh   6. care
7. differently 8. concentrate 9. late
10. advance

D

1. They have a lot of fun together.
2. There's always the danger of being laid off.
3. They'd be prepared to do a lot of overtime.
4. We'd be fine as long as we had a reasonable job.
5. He might think differently if he was a woman.

G

Word search

monotonous, overtime, steady, suit, manager, laid, excitement, promoted, paperwork, ideal, meet, prepared, hours, salary, fresh

H

Hidden message

Dear Hassan,

I've been laid off. If you hear of any good jobs, please let me know. I don't mind working hard and doing overtime. I also don't mind if the work is monotonous and there's a lot of paperwork. I just need a secure job. Tomoko.

UNIT 6

Listening/reading worksheet

B

1. commute   2. life   3. sorry
4. experience

D

drawn, glamorous, stayed, materialistic, unfriendly, gadgets

E

1. 8: many, more, materialistic, much, mentally, maybe, make, minds.
2. shallow

3. make up our minds
4. latest
5. routine

F

1. He thinks people in big cities are often unfriendly.
2. They'd be much healthier, both physically and mentally.
3. We need a chance to experience city life while we are young.

G

1. It sometimes takes hours to commute to work.
2. There aren't enough exciting opportunities in the country or small towns.
3. He thinks it's materialistic and shallow.

H

1. There are many more jobs.
3. He feels sorry for people who go to big cities.
5. We should make up our own minds about what's important in life.

Unit assessment

A

1. seat   2. pollution   3. environment
4. commute   5. routine   6. drawn
7. why   8. residential   9. unspoiled
10. bridge

D

1. The buildings around here are all made of concrete.
2. The surprising thing is that I feel lonely.
3. They spend so much time discussing the latest electronic gadgets.
4. My alarm didn't go off and I overslept.
5. The surrounding countryside is very unspoiled.

G

Word search
commute, choice, mentally, town, spend, ridiculous, glamorous, suburb, traffic, population, shallow, crowded, area, stuck, sorry

H

Hidden message
Dear Tomoko,
Don't you think you should move to a larger city? It may be overcrowded, and you may need to commute a long way, but it will be easier to find a job. And, you may find life is a lot more glamorous and stimulating. Hassan.

UNIT 7

Listening/reading worksheet

B

1. idea   2. believe   3. back
4. in

D

teamwork, cynical, true, conventional, supposed, selfish

E

1. 8: can, character, considered, cynical, cooperate, creative, conventional, created
2. made up
3. taken in by
4. conventional/unconventional, good/bad
5. made a lot of money

F

1. A
2. AB
3. His sister.

G

1. Tomoko is considered very individualistic in Japan.
2. Type A people usually cooperate with others.
3. He's never created a thing in his life.

H

1. She's more ambitious than most people.
3. They are good at teamwork.
5. They are taken in by judging people's character from their blood type.

Unit assessment

A

1. interpret   2. chance   3. come
4. considered   5. word   6. how
7. must   8. firmly   9. wavelength
10. ghost

D

1. Much of what he predicted has come true.
2. What am I supposed to be like?
3. I was taken in by what the salesman said.
4. I'm not sure what the answer is.
5. I genuinely believe in supernatural phenomena.

G

Word search

supernatural, telepathy, predict, zodiac, astrology, fortune, cynical, creative, pretty, type, around, stroke, lucky, deeply, closet

H

Hidden message
Dear Lee,
You sound so cynical! I think there's a lot of truth in things like judging our character from our blood type and predicting the future from our zodiac sign. I also deeply believe in vampires, ghosts and telepathy. Christina.

UNIT 8

Listening/reading worksheet

B

1. hardly   2. increase   3. causes
4. like

D

problems, governed, materialism, whatever, discovered, enforce

E

1. 6: predict, people, population, problem(s), prevent, police

2. it sounds like
3. From: population, materialism, social problems, crime, leisure time, how long we live, happiness, the number of robots
4. hardly anybody
5. population, social

F

1. She thinks we'll have much more leisure time.
2. It might lead to a lot of materialism and other social problems.
3. We'll learn more about what causes crime.

G

1. Science will discover how to keep people alive for hundreds of years.
2. Everybody will be much happier than now.
3. We could lose control of our (own) lives.

H

1. There'll be a terrible population problem.
3. She thinks there'll be more time to have a richer and more cultured life.
5. Everybody will be able to do whatever they like.

Unit assessment

A

1. wonder   2. made   3. unless
4. hardly   5. prevent   6. mean
7. give   8. true   9. hatched
10. know

D

1. I'll try to earn enough money to support my family.
2. She had an amazing stroke of luck.
3. That might lead to a lot of social problems.
4. He gave up hope of becoming a manager.
5. You never know what will happen next week.

G

Word search

scientists, invent, crime, unless, expect, discover, doubt, guess, works, knows, future, slight, nobody, count, alive

Teacher's Book Answers

H
Hidden message
Dear Christina,
Nobody can predict the future, and I doubt if supernatural things exist. Ghosts and vampires have been invented by superstitious people. I expect that in the future science will prove that they are just imagination. Lee.

UNIT 9

Listening/reading worksheet

B
1. rid   2. more   3. talking
4. cause

D
breathe, genuine, traffic, tax, stress, pollution, unhealthy

E
1. 9: stress, stuck, so, stressful, sometimes, say, should, stop, spoiled
2. get rid of
3. make
4. too dependent on
5. stop

F
1. They make people irritated.
2. She thinks it's fantastic to drive to a beautiful place and then get out and take a walk.
3. She thinks cars cause pollution.

G
1. Driving is one of the biggest causes of stress in our lives.
2. It's much healthier to go by car.
3. Many people become too dependent on cars.

H
1. By driving.
3. They don't do enough exercise.
5. There should be a higher tax on cars except those needed for genuine business purposes.

Unit assessment

A
1. dependent   2. down   3. get
4. stuck   5. talking   6. convince
7. lights   8. miss   9. first
10. how

D
1. I only use a car when I have to.
2. The public transportation around here is not very punctual.
3. Walking is a good way to get rid of stress.
4. Neon signs make the countryside ugly.
5. She doesn't know what she's talking about.

G
Word search
punctual, public, talking, nonsense, express, delayed, congested, dependent, irritated, fares, break, convince, service, catch, miss

H
Hidden message
Dear Karima,
You don't know what you're talking about! If there's a higher tax on cars, more people will use uncomfortable and crowded public transportation. And if the buses and trains become more popular, the fares will increase. Hassan.

UNIT 10

Listening/reading worksheet

B
1. understand 2. allowed   3. dying
4. women

D
natural, legal, antisocial, income, passive, power-ful, cancer, aware

E
1. 12: and, as, addictive, antisocial, agree, allowed, a, are, all, able, areas, aware

2. illegal
3. powerful
4. make
5. it's

F

1. She thinks it's natural that governments ban most drugs.
2. Because they get so much money from the taxes on cigarettes and because the tobacco companies are too powerful.
3. She thinks it's unnecessary to make smoking illegal.

G

1. Cigarettes are just as addictive as drugs like marijuana.
2. Governments shouldn't take all the fun out of our lives.
3. It's reasonable to have special areas for smoking.

H

1. It's difficult for him to understand why smoking is still legal.
3. We should be allowed to do a few things that are dangerous.
5. It's reasonable to discourage pregnant women from smoking.

Unit assessment

A

1. all	2. give	3. end
4. sense	5. tax	6. conspiracy
7. habit	8. temptation	9. grateful
10. mind		

D

1. Some people don't know when to stop talking.
2. Millions of people are dying of heart attacks unnecessarily.
3. It's reasonable to discourage alcoholics from drinking.
4. How long have you been feeling like this?
5. Do you mind if I cook lunch in my pajamas?

G

Word search

willpower, legal, pregnant, profit, addicted, natural, cancer, annoying, mind, temptation, antisocial, discourage, attack, passive, paid

H

Hidden message

Dear Hassan,
Driving is an unhealthy drug that too many people are addicted to. For some people, it seems to require a lot of willpower to give it up. I don't really understand why. Life is so much nicer without a car. Karima.

UNIT 11

Listening/reading worksheet

B

1. spend	2. seems	3. spoil
4. common		

D

ceremony, ridiculous, impression, comfortably, divorce, appreciate

E

1. 10: countries, ceremony(ies), clothes, crazy, children, comfortably, come, couple(s), common, course
2. traditional
3. paid
4. common
5. for

F

1. She thinks most of them are paid for by the parents.
2. She thinks we don't appreciate them.
3. She thinks they want the children to understand how important and special marriage is.

G

1. Wedding ceremonies are special family gatherings.
2. When expensive things come too easily, we

Teacher's Book Answers

don't appreciate them.
3. The parents want the couple to understand how important marriage is.

H
1. They spend a lot of money on wedding ceremonies (or honeymoons etc...).
3. She thinks it's important for married couples to build their homes gradually by themselves.
5. She thinks divorce is less common in some countries than others.

Unit assessment

A
1. opposite 2. divorce 3. unrealistic
4. ridiculous 5. natural 6. gradually
7. heart 8. future 9. suspicious
10. split

D
1. If marriages are arranged, the couples will soon separate.
2. Some people spend ridiculous amounts of money on new clothes.
3. When love comes too easily we don't appreciate it.
4. Finding a new job is not as easy as it seems.
5. We used to go out together but we split up.

G
Word search
anniversary, ridiculous, affair, fall, honeymoons, ceremony, extravagant, heart, gradually, impression, separate, romantic, split, seems, single

H
Hidden message
Dear Tomoko,
I've fallen in love! I hardly know him, but he proposed to me yesterday and we may get engaged next week. I know we should take more time to get to know each other, but I am sure I will love him forever. Jin-Sook.

UNIT 12

Listening/reading worksheet

B
1. local 2. danger 3. types
4. show

D
morally, feelings, reasonable, endangered, experiments, extinct

E
1. 7: local, looking, lot, like, less, level, least
2. horrified
3. factor
4. that
5. morally, particularly

F
1. She thinks we should accept that there is no difference between eating cows and eating whales.
2. She says that some kinds/types of whales are not on the endangered list.
3. Most of us would be horrified if somebody suggested eating a dog or a human.

G
1. Many people get upset if we eat some animals but not others.
2. Tomoko accepts that we shouldn't eat endangered species.
3. There are experiments that show that plants have feelings.

H
1. She thinks local customs and ways of looking at certain animals vary a lot.
3. He thinks it's morally wrong to eat any kind of meat.
5. He thinks most people accept that it's all right to eat plants.

Unit assessment

A

1. wrong   2. survival   3. dying
4. ways   5. difference   6. danger
7. accept   8. fish   9. away
10. straight

D

1. It's wrong to eat any animal that's in danger of becoming extinct.
2. I'm not sure whether money should be the deciding factor.
3. We've split up but there are plenty more fish in the sea.
4. The early bird catches the worm.
5. When we stayed with my relatives we had to be as quiet as a mouse.

G

Word search

endangered, experiment, evolution, nature, dying, domestic, extinct, admit, tame, fittest, species, suggested, mammal, straight, away

H

Hidden message
Dear Jin-Sook,
You're as blind as a bat! Can't you see that he's only interested in your money! He told me himself, so I got it straight from the horse's mouth. Don't worry! There are plenty more fish in the sea.
Tomoko.

UNIT 13

Listening/reading worksheet

B

1. time   2. attention   3. around
4. handling

D

solving, unsociable, technology, concentrate, world, interactive

E

1. 11: sounds, same, so, solving, something, such, shouldn't, sit, screens, spend, sure
2. puzzles
3. too, as well
4. help, be
5. handling

F

1. He thinks it helps their ability to concentrate and keep working at things.
2. He thinks they are bad for children's eyesight.
3. He thinks they used to watch TV.

G

1. He knows children who are in a world of their own.
2. He thinks children shouldn't just sit in front of their computer screens.
3. Hassan thinks their parents thought they'd all become dull and passive.

H

1. He thinks they don't know how to relate to other people.
3. He thinks they need to run around and play with each other.
5. He thinks they'll be good at handling all the new technology.

Unit assessment

A

1. virus   2. download   3. access
4. world   5. attention   6. think
7. curious   8. can't   9. check
10. wishful

D

1. She's deleted the software that caused the problem.
2. It's worth downloading anti-virus software.
3. Many children don't know how to relate to other people.
4. Computer games help children's ability to keep working at things.

Teacher's Book Answers

5. Children are very curious about what's going on around them.

G

Word search

interactive, attachment, network, unsociable, graphics, access, check, screens, download, virus, generation, technology, must, expect, dull

H

Hidden message

Dear Sonchai,

I opened an e-mail attachment yesterday, and now my computer has a virus. It crashes all the time, and some of my files have been deleted. It's driving me crazy! I don't know how to get rid of the virus. Carlos.

UNIT 14

Listening/reading worksheet

B

1. settle   2. else   3. changing
4. say

D

older, effective, qualifications, conforming, follow, experience

E

1. 8: steady, sooner, some, settle, same, society, seem, say
2. settle down
3. job, qualification, bored, older
4. be like everybody else, follow the crowd
5. there's no point in

F

1. She wants to be with people that are creative and artistic, and who aren't afraid to be different.
2. People who have steady jobs, follow society's rules, but question those rules and try to change them.
3. She thinks it doesn't get us anywhere.

G

1. She thinks it's important for each of us to be ourselves.
2. He thinks there's no need to lose our individuality.
3. She thinks they become more conservative.

H

1. She gets bored when she's with people that do the same thing every day or just want to be like everybody else.
3. They try to improve society's rules.
5. The managers don't listen.

Unit assessment

A

1. children   2. fault   3. happen
4. right   5. ourselves   6. gradually
7. point   8. age   9. generation
10. fence

D

1. She understands why older people criticize her.
2. Sooner or later I'll have to get some qualifications.
3. I'm gradually gaining the power to make changes.
4. Getting a steady job doesn't get us anywhere.
5. Trying to change her mind is like banging my head against a brick wall.

G

Word search

conservative, adolescent, conform, adult, power, fault, improve, reason, experience, settle, mature, magazine, radical, rebel, ourselves

H

Hidden message

Dear Tomoko,

I feel like an immature adolescent. I thought I was in love, but now we just argue all the time, and he finds fault in everything I do. I should have taken your advice, but I just sit on the fence and can't decide what to do. Jin-Sook.

UNIT 15

Listening/reading worksheet

B

1. together   2. effort   3. doubt
4. instead

D

true, reasonable, confidence, galleries, share, countryside

E

1. 18: ten, too, that, tour, together, travel, TV, that, true, to, them, think, there, the, try, though, they, together, tourist
2. no different from
3. get
4. make
5. go

F

1. She usually joins a tour group.
2. He likes to visit country areas.
3. Because most people don't get long vacations.

G

1. She can make a lot of new friends.
2. It's often said that travel broadens the mind.
3. There's a lot we can understand about local culture.

H

1. We have to make an effort to get to know local people.
3. She doesn't have enough confidence to go off into the countryside on her own.
5. He thinks she won't want to go back to visiting the famous tourist sights.

Unit assessment

A

1. discount   2. insurance   3. feeling
4. thing   5. own   6. bet
7. destination 8. missed   9. quiet
10. life

D

1. The cost of the vacation depends on the exchange rate.
2. I usually get jet lag after a long flight.
3. People say that travel broadens the mind.
4. I doubt if I'll be able to get a discount ticket.
5. When I take a vacation, I just like to get away and get some peace and quiet.

G

Word search
sunbathe, souvenirs, abroad, miss, destination, confidence, insurance, discount, exchange, package, local, trip, cycling, doubt, tour

H

Hidden message
Dear Jin-Sook
Why don't you take a vacation? You need to get away and have some peace and quiet. You could go to some beautiful out-of-the-way place and just relax. If you don't have enough confidence to do it, I'll come with you. Tomoko.